N
W E
S

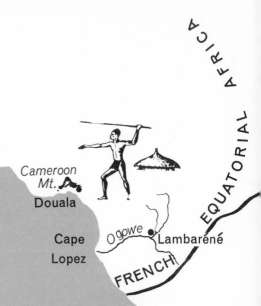

EQUATORIAL AFRICA

Cameroon
Mt. Douala

Cape
Lopez

Ogowe ● Lambaréné

FRENCH

ATLANTIC OCEAN

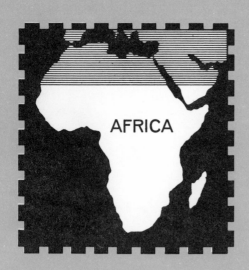

AFRICA

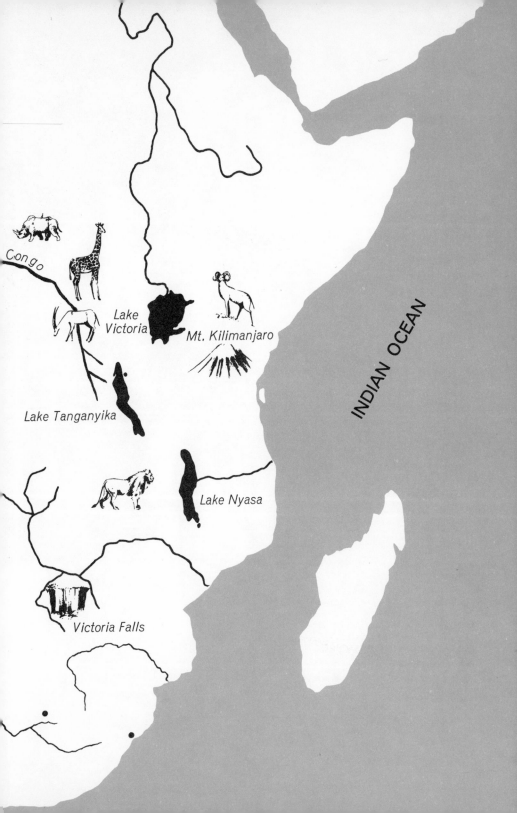

Congo

Lake
Victoria

Mt. Kilimanjaro

Lake Tanganyika

Lake Nyasa

Victoria Falls

INDIAN OCEAN

the true story of

ALBERT SCHWEITZER

HUMANITARIAN

BY JOHN MERRETT

CHILDRENS PRESS, CHICAGO

American edition published through the courtesy of
Frederick Muller Limited
London

Library of Congress Catalog Card Number: 64-12906
Copyright © in Great Britain, 1960, John Merrett
© 1964, Childrens Press
Lithographed in the U.S.A.

1956

Contents

Foreword

An International Figure 13

Alsatian Childhood 19

Poorest Boy at the Gymnasium 29

Campfire Studies 39

Momentous Decision 53

From Gunsbach to Lambaréné 61

Chicken-House Clinic 69

Stupidity of War 81

Turning Point 91

Return to Lambaréné 103

A Difficult Year 115

Jungle Hospital 123

War Touches Lambaréné 133

Author and Artist 141

Index of Place Names 142

Credits 143

Foreword

The story of Schweitzer is the story of one of the truly great men of our time—one who has lived his life for others.

His boyhood was not unusual except that he showed a great talent for music and, at nine, was playing the organ in his father's church.

At thirty, he was giving Bach concerts in many countries. He had degrees in philosophy and theology and was head of a college of a large university. He gave up all this to study medicine and then went to a remote village on the Ogowe River in French Equatorial Africa. There in a suffocating little converted chicken house he set up a one-bed hospital and began his life of service to the natives. His work was vigorous, practical and exciting. A patient might be a boatman mauled by a hippopotamus or a leper.

Characteristic of the man is the fact that he used his $30,000 Nobel Peace Prize money to combat leprosy. His reverence for life is apparent throughout his amazing story.

the true story of

ALBERT SCHWEITZER

An International Figure

On October 19, 1955, a tall, broad-shouldered old gentleman, with a shock of unruly white hair and a large, bushy mustache, was driven into the entrance of Buckingham Palace to be received by Queen Elizabeth II. The old gentleman had been summoned in order that he might receive, at the hands of the Queen, one of the highest honors which her country can bestow—the Order of Merit.

The Order of Merit, founded by Edward VII at the time of his Coronation, is awarded to very few people and, although it is such a high honor, it confers no rank or title upon its holders. The only mark of their greatness is the privilege of having the letters O.M. added to their names. Only twenty-four British men and women may be members of this Order at any one time. They are honored for one of two reasons—either for distinguished service to their country as sailors, soldiers or airmen, or because they have made great names for themselves in Science, Art or Literature.

In addition to the British members, it is possible for the Order of Merit to be awarded to eminent persons from other countries. At the present time only two people in the world who are not British are entitled to have the letters O.M. written after their names. One of them, an American, lived in the White House at Washington, D.C.—Mr. Dwight D. Eisenhower, former President of the United States of America. The other one—our shock-headed old gentleman—lives in a small bungalow in the midst of the jungle in French Equatorial Africa. His name is Albert Schweitzer and he is one of the greatest men of our day—although for very different reasons than those which bring greatness in most cases.

The Order of Merit is not the only mark of the world's esteem which has been conferred upon Albert Schweitzer. In addition to the degrees in Philosophy, Theology and Medicine of the University of Strassburg, all of which he achieved by scholarship and examination, Dr. Schweitzer has been awarded honorary degrees by Universities all over the world.

Zurich, Prague, Edinburgh, Oxford, St. Andrews, Chicago and Cambridge, in that order, have so honored him. In 1951 he became a Member of the French Academy, an honor which France bestows only upon her greatest and most illustrious sons in the spheres of Art and Letters.

But perhaps the highest honor of all those bestowed upon Dr. Schweitzer was the Nobel Peace Prize for 1952, because the Nobel Prize is open to the whole world. The winner can only be a great international figure. When Alfred Nobel, a Swedish chemist and engineer, died he left his vast fortune to a fund, with instructions that the annual interest was to be awarded in prizes to a physicist, a chemist, a writer and "the person who shall have most or best promoted the fraternity of nations." This latter, called the Peace Prize, is awarded by a committee made up of five members of the Norwegian Parliament—with the whole world from which to choose. The Prize is worth about $30,000.

In December, 1953, the ceremony of presentation of the Nobel Peace Prizes for 1952 and 1953 took place at Oslo University. The King of Norway, King Haakon, and Crown Prince Olav were present, together with many notable people from many countries. The Prize for 1953 was presented by the King to General George Marshall, of the U.S.A., for his outstanding work in helping Western Europe to economic recovery after World War II by means of what came to be known as the Marshall Plan.

The recipient of the 1952 Prize was not even present to receive the great ovation which undoubtedly would have been given him. Instead of being in the Hall of Oslo University, Dr. Schweitzer was busy working in the tropical heat of Equatorial Africa, treating the diseases of primitive natives. The French Ambassador received his Nobel Peace Prize for him and read his speech. Never before can the money which goes with this Prize have been put to a stranger use. Schweitzer said in the speech which he had written that he would spend all the money in continuing his efforts to cure 250 lepers. He would buy timber, cement and corrugated metal and extend his hospital buildings—none of the money would be spent on himself. Surely, Nobel Peace Prize money has never before been spent on corrugated metal!

I have already mentioned that Albert Schweitzer is a doctor of medicine. He has many other claims to fame. He is a great musician. Few people anywhere play the organ as well as he can and you can buy recordings which have been made of him playing the music of his favorite of all the composers —Johann Sebastian Bach. But not only can Schweitzer play the organ. He also knows all about how an organ works and how it is built. He has written books on music.

Great scholar, theologian, doctor of medicine, University professor and principal of a college, musician of outstanding ability, and author of many books, which have been translated into several languages—why did such a man bury himself in the jungle of Africa among the people who live there? There are two answers to that question. One is the deep Christian faith which Albert Schweitzer possesses—and is prepared to practice to an extent which, perhaps, few other

16

Christians would. He went to Africa to face disease, misery and primitive people in order that he might put his faith into practice. The second reason—why he chose Africa—is to be found among a group of stone figures surrounding a statue of a French admiral in the town of Colmar, France. But we must go back to the beginning of Schweitzer's life for that.

Alsatian Childhood

Albert Schweitzer was born January 14, 1875. That is a long time ago and there cannot be many people left who were alive then and could now tell us about this delicate child, born in the small town called Kayserberg, in Alsace. Fortunately, Dr. Schweitzer wrote a charming little book of his childhood memories and we can catch glimpses of his early life from it. His was just the sort of childhood that might have

19

been given to anyone and, unless he has been extremely modest, there seems to have been nothing extraordinary about his youth which might have indicated that a remarkable man was in the making. Nothing except his aptitude for music.

It would be difficult to choose (if we had any choice in the matter) a more troublous place in which to be born than Alsace in 1875. It was a province of France but, following the German victory in the Franco-Prussian War, it was ceded to Germany in 1870. Thus, to some extent, the childhood of Schweitzer was spent while his country was under foreign domination. Furthermore, Alsace is largely Roman Catholic —yet the Schweitzers were Protestants and Albert's father was a Pastor of his church. To be a member of a minority usually leaves its mark—either bitterness or defiance. There was every excuse for Schweitzer being strongly prejudiced, both nationally and in his religion. In fact, he is the most tolerant of all people. No word of complaint is ever made by him about German rule, nor does he bear any animosity towards Roman Catholicism.

It is strange how many of the world's great men have been weakly babies. There were times when Schweitzer's parents thought they would never rear him. When he was six months old his father was moved to the town of Gunsbach, still in Alsace and not far from Mulhouse. Naturally, the induction of a new Pastor brought a large gathering of people from far and near and young Albert was specially dressed up in a white frock. Nobody thought very much of the sickly-looking child however—to the great grief of his poor mother.

Very naturally some of Albert Schweitzer's earliest memories concern church. From the age of three he was taken there every Sunday and, even if he didn't understand a lot of what went on, it must have made an impression on a small child to see his father in the central position, conducting the service and preaching the sermon while all the congregation obediently listened.

The Gunsbach church had one peculiarity. It was used on Sundays by both the Roman Catholics and Protestants—at different times, of course. This dual usage sprang from a decree of Louis XIV devised to humiliate the Protestants. It stated that in any village with seven or more Catholic families, the chancel of the Protestant church must be given to them for their services. Thus young Albert watched his father preach to his Protestant flock with a background of glittering finery—an altar painted to look like gold, with tall, shining brass candlesticks and golden statues on the wall above. After Gunsbach no other church was the same. In Gunsbach Protestants and Catholics could use the same building to worship God, so there must be a great deal of similarity between them, so Schweitzer thought. So he learned religious tolerance very early.

But of all that happened in church it was the music which made the greatest impression on young Albert Schweitzer. From the beginning he loved the singing, and he did what many another young child has done—he sang, loudly. The words meant little to him and the tune even less, but he wanted to make his contribution, until the Schweitzer's maidservant, sitting next to him, decided that he must be hushed before he attracted too much attention and placed her hand over the little boy's mouth to keep him quiet!

Children often get the most remarkable ideas about church services and Albert Schweitzer was no exception. He hadn't been going for many Sundays when, on looking up at the organ, he saw a little opening at the side and a dark, hairy face looking down into the church. Schweitzer was horrified. Such a face could only belong to the devil! It must be Satan himself! Then the Pastor mounted the pulpit steps to begin his sermon and, as if by magic, the devil disappeared. Young Albert decided that his father's sermons scared the devil away—but he was back again when the closing hymn was played. Not for a long time did Albert discover that the opening was a mirror and the hairy face was a reflection of the organist, who used the mirror so that he might know the exact moment when he should start or stop playing.

When Albert Schweitzer was eight he started to take organ lessons—and his teacher was none other than old "Daddy" Iltis, whom he had formerly mistaken for the devil! But these were not his first music lessons for, when he was only five, his father started to teach him on an old square piano. Albert quickly picked up the art, but he didn't like ordinary practicing from music. His great joy was to make up melodies for himself and so well did he manage that he gave his teacher at the village school a surprise. It happened like this.

During singing lessons the teacher first of all picked out the tune with one finger on the harmonium. One day Albert asked her about this and wanted to know why she didn't play with both hands. The teacher, perhaps a little amused by a seven-year-old asking such a question, asked him whether he could do so. She got the surprise of her life. Albert sat down and played a hymn right through, with full harmony! Next singing lesson, however, the teacher still played with only one finger. Albert couldn't understand why—till he came to the obvious conclusion. *He* could play better than his teacher! The thought gave him little pleasure. He wished he had not displayed his skill the day before. It looked like "showing-off." However, his teacher didn't feel that way about it and she was as pleased and proud as his parents when, only two years later, Albert Schweitzer was able to play for the entire service on the church organ.

But we must not picture this boy as the Pastor's son, the studious and clever young musician. The truth is, music apart, young Schweitzer was far from being the brightest boy in the class—and he hated the idea of being regarded as a cut above the others, just because his father was the Pastor. There was, for instance, the time when Albert had a new overcoat. True, it was made from an old one of his father's, but the village boys had no overcoats and neither had their fathers. They couldn't afford them. Albert rebelled against wearing that coat. The tailor who altered it started his dislike by saying, "By Jove, Albert, now you're a regular gentleman!"

After that there was a perpetual struggle between Albert and his parents whenever it was cold enough for a coat to be worn. Often he was punished for refusing to put it on because, even at that early age, he was a true democrat. He wanted no privileged position. Like the village boys, he wore wooden clogs and fingerless mittens on weekdays. Leather boots were for Sunday wear only. When his mother took him to Strassburg to buy him a fine, new sailor's hat he would have none of it because the village boys had to appear in old brown caps, pulled well down over their ears. So it had to be a similar cap for Albert—to the disgust of the shopkeeper and his mother.

But it was all of no avail. The village boys took not the slightest notice of all Albert Schweitzer's efforts to be one of them—and when they quarreled with him, they taunted him with being "one of the gentry."

One side of Albert Schweitzer's boyhood character will be understood by many of us. Although he was inclined to shyness and quietness in most things, he had a strong sense of the ridiculous and it was very easy to make him laugh. Such children are always at the mercy of their fellows. It is always a great joke to be able to make someone laugh at the wrong time, and that is just what Albert's companions did. As a result he earned a nickname—given to him by his schoolmaster, Pastor Schaffler, who gave religious instruction. Not unnaturally, the nickname therefore came from the Bible. It was "Isaac"—and you will find that it means "he who laughs."

Our picture of Schweitzer as a boy would not be complete

without a mention of his great fondness for animals. Here again, we have a trait which continued unchanged throughout his life. Schweitzer has always believed in what he calls the Sanctity of Life—the right which all creatures have to that one thing which man can take, but cannot give back— life itself. When he was quite young, Albert Schweitzer saw an old horse being taken—not without cruelty—to be slaughtered because it could not work any more. The anguish he suffered from seeing that poor, old horse remained with him for a very long time. He could not get it out of his mind. So deep was this feeling for what we sometimes call dumb animals that Schweitzer, when very young, decided that if we mentioned people in our prayers there was no reason why animals should be excluded. He therefore included them.

Once or twice this love for animals brought difficulties. There was the time when he and young Henry Brasch made slingshots for themselves, and Henry decided it would be a fine idea to go and shoot birds. Albert thought quite differently, but he could not say so for fear Henry Brasch would laugh at him. He could see things from the birds' viewpoint and the very idea of maiming or killing birds simply for the sake of so-called "sport" horrified him. Some way of saving the birds had to be found and it was the church bell which provided the inspiration. As the two boys reached a large tree —leafless because it was early springtime—they saw it was full of birds, singing as birds will at that time. Henry Brasch put a stone in his sling and signaled to Albert to do the same. Whether they would have hit any of the birds is another matter—Albert was sure that one of the singers was bound to be a victim. Just at that moment the church bell started ringing in the valley below. Albert regarded it as a sign from Heaven so he jumped up, shouted, waved his arms—and shooed all the birds out of the tree. Then he turned and ran for home as hard as he could go—afraid, perhaps, that the stone in Henry Brasch's sling might have found its mark on himself!

But young Albert was not always the model child. Once in Colmar—the town where his godparents lived—he and another boy, after being warned that they must not go near the river, deliberately went there, untied a boat and set off for a voyage of their own. They were discovered by the boat's owner and there was plenty of trouble when they got back.

Many a normal boy has found that one of the greatest nuisances of his young life is his hair. Grownups will insist that hair should be neatly parted and tidy, and not everyone is born with tidy hair. Albert Schweitzer certainly wasn't.

His unruly shock of hair was a challenge to the family's maidservant. She tried everything to make that hair lie flat —brushing it till the boy thought he had no hair left, combing it with all the energy she had or trying to stick it down with some thick, sticky brilliantine. Half an hour later it was as bad as ever so then she would resort to abuse—"Unruly without, unruly within . . ." and similar remarks. Young Albert was inclined to get worried about it when it reached that stage; at least he did until he saw the picture of St. John in Colmar Museum. In the picture St. John had a shock of fair hair, and Albert Schweitzer decided that if St. John had to put up with unruly hair, then so could he.

When he was ten years old Albert Schweitzer left home and went to live with his Great-uncle Louis and Great-aunt Sophie in order to begin his secondary education. His school was the Gymnasium at Mulhausen. If that word conjures up visions of scholars doing their lessons on parallel bars or swinging from ropes, I must explain that the old meaning of Gymnasium was "a school for the higher branches of literature and science." The educational standard of the Gymnasium was high and, because he was a Pastor's son, Albert was entitled to receive his schooling free.

Mulhausen, a fairly large town, was too far from Gunsbach for daily travel and so, at that early age, Schweitzer had to leave his beloved countryside and go to a large and gloomy house in the middle of town. (I have deliberately called the town Mulhausen and Albert's school the Gymnasium because those were the names by which he knew them. Then, they were in Germany and Albert Schweitzer was a German subject. In 1918, when Alsace became French again, Mulhausen became Mulhouse and the Gymnasium turned French and was called the Lycée.)

Poorest Boy at the Gymnasium

Life with Great-uncle Louis and Great-aunt Sophie was somewhat irksome for a boy of ten. Great-uncle Louis was in charge of all the primary schools in Mulhausen and his wife was a former school mistress. Theirs was a disciplined and extremely orderly house. Everything was governed by rules and each day ran in strict accordance with a timetable. Albert had his meals at set times, went to school at the correct moment, kept exact hours for piano practice and went to bed on the dot. In his spare time he read everything he could lay his hands on. His aunt tried to exercise some sort of control. She considered that he didn't read properly or with full understanding—he was too apt to skim through books. Most of all, she disapproved his reading the newspapers. She said they were not for children because they contained such things as murder cases.

Eventually, with Albert protesting that his chief interest in the papers was the political news, the matter was referred to Uncle Louis. As an educationist he decided on an examination—with European politics as the subject. He started with the ruling princes and prime ministers of the Balkan states, went on to the French Government and finished with speeches in the Reichstag in Berlin. Albert passed this oral test, held during suppertime, brilliantly—and was allowed to read the papers every day, at stated times, of course. Moreover, his uncle treated him as a young man of the world and actually discussed politics with him at meal times. Naturally, Albert read the political news with a critical eye from that time. He wanted to maintain his position with his uncle— but he also read the stories in the Library Supplement!

I suppose that all of us take comfort occasionally when we are told that some of the world's greatest men were poor scholars. Up to a point, Albert Schweitzer is a good example. He started badly—but he made great improvements. Indeed, he started so badly at the Gymnasium that he was in danger of expulsion! The Principal sent for Pastor Schweitzer and told him pretty plainly that unless there was a great improvement in Albert's work, he would have to leave. This was a matter of great concern. Poor pastors were grateful enough to have their sons educated free of charge at good schools. It would have been not only a great disgrace to be asked to take a pupil away, but would also raise the question of where the money was coming from for schooling.

The trouble with Albert Schweitzer was that he was too much of a dreamer and, consequently, his work suffered. He was even oblivious of the distress caused by his bad reports.

Then, just when everything seemed at its blackest and Albert's mother had wept over her son's latest and worst report, a change came. A new teacher, called a form master, Dr. Wehmann, appeared. Unlike some of the other masters, he took the greatest trouble over his subjects and his pupils. He was methodical. Each lesson was carefully prepared; the master knew where he would start and finish and how much ground he would cover. Albert's generous nature responded straight away. Here was a man who took great trouble and young Schweitzer resolved to show his appreciation. His next report caused not tears but happiness. He was one of the best pupils in his class, and continued to be.

He also had trouble with music. Here, however, the reasons were different. The true musician possesses great feeling for his music. Albert was a musician but he hesitated to show what he felt before his teacher. This teacher, Eugen Munch, was organist at a big church in Mulhausen. He loved music, so you may imagine his feelings about the boy who preferred to strum improvisations of his own and who rattled off, in most unsympathetic manner, the works of the great composers. Munch regarded this boy Albert Schweitzer with despair. What was the good of wasting time trying to teach the works of the great musicians to such an unfeeling young rascal?

One day Eugen Munch could stand no more. He had given Schweitzer one of Mozart's sonatas for his practice—Mozart, whose music possesses an almost ethereal wistfulness and beauty. The boy had practiced it badly—and played it worse. When the dull, wooden performance finished, Munch became angry. He opened a book of Mendelssohn's *Songs without Words*, one of which was to be the next practice.

"You don't deserve to have such beautiful music given you to play," he said. "You'll spoil Mendelssohn's music for me just like you spoil everything else. If you've no feeling for music, I can't give it to you!"

Here, indeed, was a challenge to Albert Schweitzer. Of course he loved this sort of music—he'd never dared to show how much. He went away with the *Songs without Words* and, for a whole week, he practiced the chosen piece. He even worked out the best fingering and wrote it on the music. When the next visit to Herr Munch came, after going through his exercises and scales, the boy played the Mendelssohn piece. He played with his fingers, but he put his very soul into it. His teacher listened. No word was spoken and then, as the last notes faded into silence, Eugen Munch gently moved the boy to one side and played to him another of those *Songs without Words.* Henceforth there was an understanding between master and pupil. There were no more accusations about lack of feeling. Beethoven followed Mendelssohn and then came Bach, the composer who was to mean more than all others to Albert Schweitzer.

Of all the results which followed from that rendering of Mendelssohn none pleased young Schweitzer more than the news that he was to have lessons on the magnificent organ in St. Stephen's Church at Mulhausen. An organ with three keyboards and sixty-two stops! Albert had been playing the organ at Gunsbach church since he was nine years old—but the Gunsbach organ could not compare with this one. He was a diligent pupil. When he was sixteen he was allowed to take the place of his master, Eugen Munch, at church services and soon afterwards he was entrusted with the organ accompaniment of Brahm's *Requiem,* when it was sung by the church choir. Schweitzer says of that moment that he tasted for the first time the joy of letting the organ send its own glorious, swelling tones to intermingle with the voices of the choir and the instruments of the orchestra.

It might seem to us that, between his greatly improved position in his class and the satisfaction and joy of his music, Albert Schweitzer must have been very happy during those years at the Gymnasium. This was not entirely so for there was one sorrow and anxiety to face which might well have broken boys of lesser spirit. The Schweitzer family was very poor. There were four other children and, to make matters worse, their father was ill for a long time. Money was very

scarce indeed and every possible economy had to be practiced—even to the extent of going short of things like butter.

One of the effects of this poverty was that Albert's position
at school was exactly the reverse of what it was at Gunsbach.
Then he had been in the privileged position; they had called
him "one of the gentry." Now he was the boy in his class
who had least—and boys are usually quick to look down on
their poverty-stricken fellows. One autumn Albert's mother,
realizing that his winter suit had become much too small,
said that he needed another. Albert said his old suit would
do well enough but, when he got back to Mulhausen, he had
to shiver through the winter in his light summer suit because
he simply could not get into his old winter one. He felt he
would rather face the sneers of the other boys than add to
his parents' worries. Maybe we can understand from this
something of the reason for his reluctance to reveal his real
feelings to his music master. Not many people today possess
that sort of pride. It takes a lot of courage to face the world
when you are only fourteen and the poorest boy in the school.

But better times came. A son of a former minister at Gunsbach, who had made money as an engineer, died and left his
house to the parish as a residence for the Pastor. It was a
tremendous improvement on the old house and Pastor
Schweitzer's health began to improve as soon as the family
moved. In addition, a distant relative left them some money,
so all their worries came to an end. Albert's schooling progressed and history and science became his two favorite subjects. His music went from strength to strength so that he

decided to make it one of his subjects at the University. The other two were to be Theology (so that he might follow his father's example) and Philosophy. But before he could go to the University he had to pass a pretty stiff examination at the Gymnasium. Nobody thought Albert would have much difficulty in passing but things nearly turned out disastrously —and all because of a pair of trousers! It happened like this.

The examination was conducted orally. The School Commissioner from Strassburg came specially for the occasion to preside over the questioning. He was an important figure and his sternness was in keeping with his importance. On the great day it was the custom for all the young men taking the examination to dress in their most formal clothes—usually a frock coat and black trousers. Albert had a frock coat—an old one which had been given to him by one of his relatives—but no black trousers. He had no money to buy a pair so it was arranged that he might borrow those of his Great-uncle Louis. Unfortunately it was assumed that the trousers would fit, even though Great-uncle Louis was short and stout and Albert was tall and thin. Albert put them on for the first time on the day of the examination. The result was ridiculous. Even when his suspenders were lengthened with string, the trousers were halfway up to his knees and there was a big gap between the top of them and his vest! Worst of all was the rear view. There was room and to spare in the seat!

Albert Schweitzer's appearance caused riotous hilarity at the Gymnasium, where everyone saw the joke except, unfortunately, the School Commissioner. He realized that Albert was the center of all the fun so he decided he would personally examine this joker. In the beginning the questioning went badly for Schweitzer. He even had to admit he didn't know some of the answers to questions although the Principal of the Gymnasium did his best for him. Then, with things looking pretty black, the questions turned to history. This was Albert's own special subject and his answers delighted the examiner. In the end the two of them, School Commissioner and pupil, discussed various historical points with the greatest friendliness. Albert Schweitzer passed his examination and earned his certificate, with a special word of commendation from the Commissioner himself on his knowledge of history.

And so his Gymnasium days ended. Albert Schweitzer, at the age of nineteen, left his great-uncle and great-aunt at Mulhausen with many regrets. He was now to become a student at Strassburg University.

Life must have seemed very good to Albert Schweitzer in the year 1893. He had succeeded in his passing-out examination at the Gymnasium at Mulhausen, he began his studies at the Strassburg University, which was then making a great reputation for itself, and he went to Paris for the first time. The visit to Paris must have been a great event and, in October 1893, the city was *en fete* in celebration of an alliance with Russia. Everywhere there were parades and celebrations, but none of them made such an impression on

Albert Schweitzer as his meeting with Charles Maurice Widor. You may well ask who Widor was and why he meant so much to Schweitzer. The answer is to be found in the one word—Music.

Widor was already famous when Albert Schweitzer went to him with an introduction from his uncle, with whom Albert was staying in Paris. Firstly, he was organist at one of the most famous churches in Paris, the church of St. Sulpice, which is almost as big as Notre Dame Cathedral, and he was also a well-known composer. Widor was in great demand as a teacher of music and normally he took only students from the Paris Conservatoire. Something about young Albert Schweitzer appealed to him, however. Maybe it was his playing, or it might have been because of Schweitzer's passionate fondness for the music of Johann Sebastian Bach for, at that time, Bach was comparatively little known—but Widor knew and admired his music. Whatever it was, Widor made Albert Schweitzer a very proud young man when he agreed to take him as a pupil, and later they became close friends.

Campfire Studies

Back in Strassburg after his visit to Paris, Schweitzer was enrolled as a student at St. Thomas's College, which stands in one of the beautiful old parts of the city, on the banks of the River Ill and surrounded by lovely old houses. Schweitzer made an early impression at his College by arriving one day on a bicycle. In 1893 it was not thought proper for young men studying for the church to ride such new-fangled frivolities as bicycles! Bicycles were new then and Schweitzer could remember the first one ever to come to Gunsbach. Word went round that one of these new machines had arrived at the inn, where its rider was taking refreshment. Soon almost everyone in Gunsbach was gathered outside and they watched with astonishment when the rider came out, mounted and rode off. Albert had always wanted a bicycle after that and, during his second year at the Gymnasium, he saved enough to buy a second-hand one. It cost more than $50.00, which was a lot of money then. Fortunately, Pastor Schweitzer was broadminded and did not object to cycling—even though some of the folks of Gunsbach though it rather wicked.

When Albert Schweitzer arrived at St. Thomas's on his bicycle he was seen by the Principal, Professor Erichson. The sight of a student riding through the gateway was something of a surprise to him but Professor Erichson was not narrowminded. He told Schweitzer it was lucky for him that the old Principal, Professor Reuss, was dead because Reuss in his day would not even allow any student to ride a horse.

Throughout Albert Schweitzer's life one great quality has been evident—he possesses the courage of his convictions. He has never been content to accept a thing because it is written or taught and, when his studies have led him to new ideas which disagree with what is taught, he has never been afraid to state his viewpoint. Something of that sort happened soon after he went to Strassburg. His first year, so he says, was "spoiled" by having to study for an examination in Hebrew. This subject is essential because students in theology must be able to read the Scriptures in the language in which some of them were first written. He found it tough going but he managed to pass his first examination less than six months after entering St. Thomas's and that spurred him on to obtaining a sound knowledge of Hebrew. He attended other lectures during that first winter and those given by Professor Holtzmann on the Gospels of Matthew, Mark and Luke particularly interested him and set him thinking.

On April 1st, 1894, Albert Schweitzer joined the German Army. Every young German had to put in one year's service and, of course, this applied to Alsatians as well. Luckily, soldiering did not entirely interfere with his studies. His regiment was stationed near the University and, thanks to the kindness and understanding of a certain Captain Krull, Schweitzer was given time off to attend lectures at 11 a.m. daily, after his military work was finished. Schweitzer's one aim during that summer was to pass an examination in the autumn and so obtain a scholarship at the University. The University authorities made allowances for young men doing their military service. Instead of the normal three subjects for the scholarship they were required to take only one. Schweitzer decided that he would take for his subject the Gospels of Matthew, Mark and Luke (sometimes known as the Synoptic Gospels because of their similarity) as they had been the subject of Professor Holtzmann's lectures.

During the late autumn of 1894, and not long before the examination, Schweitzer's regiment went on maneuvers in Lower Alsace, a long way from Strassburg. It was impossible to attend lectures so Albert packed a Greek Testament in his haversack and studied it closely during any spare moments. The open-air life was greatly to his liking. Living in a tent and spending every day out in the country was a great joy to him. In the evenings, when his fellow soldiers were sleeping or out enjoying themselves, he was busy poring over his Testament. He was very anxious that he should do well in his examination and so show his appreciation of Professor Holtzmann's teaching.

Those campfire studies had a strange result—one which, no doubt, seems to be a peculiar way of showing appreciation of what Professor Holtzmann had done for his pupil. Schweitzer gradually came to the conviction that he could not agree with his teacher on a number of vital points. Disagreement with one's teacher is a bold step to take, unless one is very certain of the reasons—and, even then, to express disagreement might well be a short cut to failing the examination. There must have been great conflict in young Schweitzer's mind as the examination drew near. He wanted to pass; yet he was not the person who could be untrue to himself. If he was convinced, then he was certain to express his beliefs honestly.

As it turned out, he need have had no worries. Professor Holtzmann, a very kindly, good-natured man, asked only straightforward and relatively easy questions because he felt sorry for young men whose studies were interrupted by military duties. Schweitzer passed his examination but did not forsake his ideas as to where he thought his teachers were wrong. Indeed it was these very doubts which set him on the

42

way to writing one of his first books—a book which caused much argument (some people were even shocked by it) and one which is still widely read and studied. The story of this book should be told, even though it occurs a little later in Schweitzer's life than the period we are now relating. It will help us to understand the man.

Many students of the New Testament think that St. Mark is the oldest of the four Gospels. They base this conclusion upon a study of the material and the style of writing. If this is so, then it is likely that the Gospels of Matthew and Luke were, to some extent, copies of the earlier book. Indeed, only 31 of the 661 verses in the Gospel of St. Mark are not repeated in one form or another in Matthew and Luke. This was the teaching of Professor Holtzmann and he held that one could only fully understand the life and work of Jesus by reading St. Mark's Gospel.

Schweitzer accepted this until, while spending a rest day in the middle of army maneuvers, he concentrated on the tenth and eleventh chapters of Matthew. Here he found items of the greatest importance, which are not recorded in the Gospel of St. Mark. He decided that perhaps this Marcan theory might not be correct after all and he began to consider how much we really know, as true history, concerning the life of Jesus Christ. In 1906 these thoughts finally found expression in Schweitzer's famous book, *The Quest of the Historical Jesus*. In this book he summarizes all the famous Lives of Christ, written in modern times, and draws his conclusions. There are people who have been uncertain of—even opposed to—what Schweitzer has to say, but his answer to them is clear and honest—"Faith which refuses to face facts is not faith." There is no use in closing our eyes to historical facts for the sake of holding on to a blind faith. Indeed, as we shall see, Schweitzer's life and faith have been in the closest accord with the teachings of Christ.

Today it is generally accepted that much that is written in Scripture is not to be taken literally— it is the teaching which lies behind these stories which matters. It is easy to say that now. It took a lot of courage to do so fifty or sixty years ago.

At about the age of twenty-one Albert Schweitzer made up his mind as to what he would do with his life. His military service was finished, he was very happily engaged at the University, working for the two degrees of Theology and Philosophy at the same time, and he was studying music as well. Holidays, when they came, were delightfully spent at the new Pastor's house at Gunsbach. He was at home when he made up his mind, on a beautiful morning during the Whitsun holiday. It seemed to him that he could not continue to enjoy such a happy life while all around him there was sorrow, anxiety and suffering. What should he do about it? In some way the answer came. He would continue with his work and studies until he was thirty. Then, in a way which he would understand later, he would devote the rest of his life to helping other people. Schweitzer says that this glimpse into the future left him happier than ever—inwardly happy. He had often puzzled over the words of Christ—

"Whosoever would save his life shall lose it, and whosoever shall lose his life for My sake and the Gospel's shall save it." Their meaning was now plain.

In the spring of 1898 came Schweitzer's first big examination in theology. He passed and was awarded a scholarship worth about $300.00 a year for six years. For the rest of that summer he worked hard at philosophy and then went to Paris to continue at the Sorbonne, and, of course, to take more music lessons from his friend Widor. He had not neglected his music in Strassburg. The organist at St. William's Church and conductor of the Bach concerts was Ernest Munch— brother of Schweitzer's music teacher in Mulhouse. While still a student, Schweitzer was allowed to play the organ parts for these Bach concerts.

In Paris Schweitzer found that he did not like the teaching methods at the Sorbonne so he continued his studies at his lodgings. He had to work very hard because he was giving a lot of his time to his music lessons. Widor taught him on the organ and he took lessons from two separate teachers on the piano. It was a bit awkward because these two disagreed with each other's ideas, so Schweitzer had to be careful to conceal that he was the pupil of both! These were times of some hardship. Not only did Schweitzer often study far into the night, he also had barely enough to eat because he had very little money. Widor knew this and often came to the rescue. When an organ lesson was finished he would take his young pupil to one of the excellent Paris restaurants and give him a good meal.

From Paris Schweitzer went to Berlin—still studying philosophy. Even so, he couldn't resist music, and especially organ music. He found that while Berlin catered better for the scholar and had a more efficient University, the church organs and organists of Paris were far superior to those in Berlin. Schweitzer was interested not only in organ music but also in the actual construction of organs. He knew many of the old organ builders and he was convinced that the organs built by the old craftsmen were far superior to the giant, factory-made instruments. He had only to hear of an old organ being badly treated or threatened by replacement with a new factory-made one and he would do everything in his power to save the old instrument—write letters, go and see people and use every persuasion. He became a real expert on organ construction and wrote an essay, which was published, on the subject. His knowledge was recognized and by his efforts many an old organ was saved from destruction or alteration, which would have left little of its original character.

At twenty-four Albert Schweitzer became a Doctor of Philosophy and two years later he passed his licentiate of theology. The second examination was passed in typical manner. As was mentioned earlier, he held a scholarship worth $300.00 a year in theology. He could continue to get this amount—it wasn't princely but it helped considerably— for six years but, at the end of that time, he had either to pass the examination or return all the money. That was a challenge —but Schweitzer made things even more difficult for himself. He had a friend, Jager, a brilliant student, and Schweitzer felt   that if only   he could pass   his theology examination he could give up his scholarship before the six years were up and so let Jager have a shot at winning it. He worked hard and attempted the examination only just over two years after he won the scholarship—thus cutting short his time by almost four years. He passed—but it was a near thing for he had worked so hard at the main subjects that some of the lesser ones were not so well covered, particularly those which concerned the writers of hymns. A dreadful thing happened as a result. One of the examiners asked who had written a certain hymn. Schweitzer didn't know and gave the excuse that the hymn was too unimportant for him to remember. In modern terms he had "dropped a brick!" The hymn was written by a very famous poet named Spitta—and the examiner who asked the question was Professor Freidrich Spitta, his son!

Unfortunately, Schweitzer's sacrifice for his friend Jager was in vain. It is true Jager won the scholarship, but he made no use of it and became a schoolmaster. Schweitzer could have had those other four years and—what he would have particularly liked—visited England and an English University.

Schweitzer, now a full-fledged curate, was appointed to the Church of St. Nicholas in Strassburg at a salary of $25.00 per month. His chief responsibility was to take the children's services, which gave him great pleasure. His method of preaching was that of his father—a short, friendly, intimate talk. The children liked the new curate but, as time went on, he was given the job of preaching to the adults as well—and some of them didn't consider they were getting a proper sermon unless it was a long one. One old lady actually complained to his superior about the shortness of his sermons—an unheard-of thing today, I'm sure! His defense was typical.

"Tell her," he said, "that I am only a poor curate who stops talking when he finds he has no more to say about his text."

Pastor Knittel smiled, gave his "poor curate" a gentle reprimand and ordered him to preach for at least twenty minutes in future.

Many men, having arrived at the position of Schweitzer, might consider that early struggles were over and the way was now open to a straightforward career in the church. Indeed, Schweitzer had many other interests. He still had his music and he also received an appointment as a teacher at the University. He lived, at small expense, in one of the University hostels and he was very happy. There undoubtedly must have been a strong temptation to renounce that resolve to give up everything when he was thirty. Indeed, he might salve his conscience by saying that as a curate of the church he was fulfilling his resolution. But Albert Schweitzer never took the easy path. Let us move on and see how his destiny was revealed to him.

At thirty Albert Schweitzer was famous in many fields. Two years before his scholarship had received full recognition when he became the youngest-ever Principal of St. Thomas's College in the University of Strassburg. The position carried a salary of $500.00 a year and excellent quarters in the beautiful old building. The salary may not sound very high to us now but, in 1903, it was quite appreciable. In addition, he received fees as a lecturer and he was in demand everywhere as an organist of the first importance.

As if all these were not enough, Schweitzer was known all over the world as an author. There were his books on religious subjects, written in German. Schweitzer has always regarded German as his mother tongue, though both he and his family always corresponded in French. In addition to these books, he was encouraged by Widor to write a short essay on the musical works of their mutual favorite, Bach.

By 1905 he had finished his book; over 450 pages, written in French. It wasn't easy to spend your whole day talking and lecturing in German and then, during the evenings, write a book in French. The book was a tremendous success and Schweitzer was asked to produce a German translation. He started it, found it impossible to translate his French thoughts into German words, discovered more material he wanted to include and, to the astonishment of his publishers, presented them with a book of over 850 pages!

Add to all this work—lecturing, preaching, writing other books, playing the organ—the interest in organ building and going round to look at old organs threatened by destruction—and you have a very busy man indeed. Some of his organ recitals were given in other countries—Germany, Spain and Britain—and he used his long train journeys for such things as preparing his sermons. But Schweitzer never lost sight of the fact that this busy life he enjoyed so much would come to an end. As the age of thirty approached he began to wonder more and more what he was destined to do to fulfil his promise to devote himself to those people who most needed help.

It is not easy to be patient in the face of something which is going to change your life completely. Schweitzer had promised that he would follow the new path which would turn his life into one of service to others when he became thirty. He was getting near the time—and still nothing had revealed itself. He did what most of us would. He made efforts to find what he should do and an early idea was that of taking a special interest in the poor. With others from the University, he embarked on what we would call social work—visiting needy families and then trying to get rich people to subscribe money to help with the relief work. Schweitzer did not enjoy the latter. Begging for money was to him a most unpleasant task, but he did it, nevertheless. One of the students who helped with this work was the daughter of a professor at Strassburg University. Her name was Helene Bresslau and her father was head of the History Department. Helene was to become a teacher at the University but her real interest was in social work. Like Albert Schweitzer, she wanted to help to relieve want and suffering.

A real opportunity seemed to put itself into Schweitzer's way a little late. An orphanage was burned down and all the children were left homeless. Schweitzer offered to take several of them, make a home for them and bring them up at his own expense. But the authorities, as is so often the case even today, would not hear of it. They required that the orphans should be kept in an institution and, once more, Schweitzer was disappointed.

Great events often have small beginnings. Nowhere, perhaps, is that truth better told than in the Old Testament story when Elijah waited on the mountain top for a message from God. There came a mighty wind, an earthquake and a great fire—but the message was not in any of them. Then came that for which Elijah waited—a still, small voice—and he knew what he should do.

Momentous Decision

One evening Albert Schweitzer went into his study to work.
Among the papers on his desk was a small magazine which
someone had left for him to glance through. It was the
Journal of the Paris Missionary Society—a Protestant organization which was conducting an uphill, disheartening struggle against poverty and disease in Africa.

Schweitzer read how desperately doctors, missionaries and

teachers were needed in French Equatorial Africa. As he read, a chord in his memory was touched and he was back, as a child, in the old town of Colmar. In the center of the town stands a piece of statuary which commemorates Admiral Bruat—a French sailor and a great traveler. Surrounding the Admiral are the figures of people from many parts of the world, one of them being an African Negro. Little Albert had always been fascinated by that Negro's carved face. It looked so sad. Now, as he read of the great need which existed in Equatorial Africa, he understood that sadness, and he knew what he would do. He could be a missionary and a teacher, but that was not enough. He would be a doctor, too, and then he could really help.

Breaking the news of this decision was one of the hardest things that Schweitzer ever had to do. Very few people understood, or even attempted to do so. When Schweitzer wrote to his various friends, they tried very hard to dissuade him. Widor in Paris, his academic friends in Berlin, the authorities at Strassburg University, they all added their protests. They argued that Schweitzer was throwing away all his wonderful talents, that Europe needed him as much as Africa and that he was going to one of the unhealthiest places in the world and might not live for long in Equatorial Africa. He patiently explained to them that he must go. Only his family—and they were worried about the risks to his health— and Helene Bresslau understood. Helene understood because her own life was bound up with that of Albert Schweitzer. Six years after he made his great decision they were married.

Meantime, Helene took up a career in nursing so that she might accompany him to Africa and help in the great work for humanity which he had chosen.

It was a strange experience for the Head of one of the Colleges in Strassburg University to commence studies, sitting in lecture rooms with young first-year students, but it was the beginning of the road towards becoming a Doctor of Medicine for Albert Schweitzer. There were difficulties. As a Professor of the University, Schweitzer could only attend lectures as a visitor and was not permitted to take the examinations. In the end the University authorities found a way round— an indication of how highly they regarded their colleague.

Despite the hard work at his medical studies, Schweitzer continued to lecture on theology, to preach in his church on Sundays and to play the organ. Indeed, he was under promise to play the organ parts for all the concerts of the Paris Bach Society, and that meant journeying to Paris several times each winter. He gave recitals in Barcelona, too. Few men could have continued under such strain but he had to have the money to keep himself while he studied medicine. He no longer had his salary as Principal of St. Thomas's College and although the University authorities most generously charged him no fees for his medical lectures, he had to live. The money from the organ recitals was badly needed.

No few short paragraphs could ever describe the seven years which Albert Schweitzer spent studying to be a doctor of medicine. He worked as few men could work; he had excellent health and a strong constitution and, but for those two great blessings, he could never have succeeded. There were times when utter weariness nearly defeated him. When those days came he would leave his lectures and go to the organ loft in St. William's Church. There, with Ernest Munch, he would spend an hour playing or listening to the music of Bach. That enabled him to go on. Schweitzer's own words about those little musical respites show us just what they meant to him. He wrote, "Oh! the healing power of that man (Bach)! I calmed down again and got back my equilibrium."

It wasn't long before the other medical students—the young men who, at first, must have been somewhat overawed at having the Principal of one of the Colleges sitting alongside them—took him as one of themselves and gave him all the help they could. About two and a half years after Schweitzer's medical studies had begun he was faced with a tough examination in anatomy, physiology, and the natural sciences. His fellow pupils decided that he wasn't going the right way about his studies and that he might fail. They decided to take him in hand and they made him join what was called a "cramming club." There they studied the sort of questions likely to be asked in the examination, and crammed for all they were worth. When the examination did come, Schweitzer, though extremely weary, managed to do far better than he had expected and passed with flying colors!

The end of this long, hard road came for Albert Schweitzer in October, 1911. This was the State Medical Examination and he had earned the fee for entrance during the previous month by playing the organ at a Musical Festival at Munich.

For nearly three months Schweitzer battled through the various parts of the examination, the last one—Surgery—being in December. As he left the hospital that evening he could scarcely realize that his years of almost unbearable struggle were over. There remained only the written thesis for the Degree of Doctor of Medicine; characteristically, Schweitzer took a most unusual subject.

There have been writers in the past who have advanced the theory that Jesus Christ suffered from some kind of mental unbalance—a disease known to medical science as paranoia, which causes its victims to suffer from mistaken ideas of grandeur or persecution. To those of us who are Christians this theory seems blasphemously impossible—but Schweitzer felt that it should be disproved by facts, from all the scientific evidence there is, as well as by faith. He set out to do this, after making a close study of this particular mental disease, and his thesis explains clearly that there can be no basis for the theory. Thus he combined his knowledge of theology and his newly-acquired medical training.

There was still more to be done before Dr. Schweitzer was ready to go to Africa. He gave up his lecturing at Strassburg University and his position at St. Nicholas's Church in the spring of 1912. Both were sad partings. In fact he was so upset at the thought of leaving these two places which he loved so much that he tried, as far as he could, to avoid even passing by them. His last sermon to his congregation came from the words which he always used to close a service—"The peace of God which passeth all understanding, keep your hearts and minds in Christ Jesus." We may be sure that many of his hearers were as moved as he.

From Strassburg he went to Paris to study tropical medicine—a special subject for one who is going to practice in hot countries. With him went his wife and, in between his studies, they commenced the tremendous task of buying all the instruments, bandages and dressings, drugs and medicines necessary for running a hospital. He had resolved to be in a position to go to the Paris Missionary Society with an offer to establish and run the hospital himself. Many people helped to raise the money. His congregation at Strassburg, the Bach Society in Paris, which gave a special concert, the German professors in Strassburg (even though the hospital was to be in French territory—and their gesture moved Schweitzer deeply for that reason), the churches in Alsace and even places as far distant as Le Havre. All of them subscribed until there was enough for what was needed.

With his medical degree, his knowledge of tropical diseases and his funds sufficient to equip a complete hospital, Schweitzer went to the Paris Missionary Society with an offer to serve in its mission field. The place he selected was Lambaréné, 200 miles up the River Ogowe and only a few miles south of the Equator, near the west coast of Africa. Not everyone in the Society was grateful for— nor even disposed to accept—this most generous offer, even though a medical mission was so badly needed at Lambaréné. The reason for this reluctance had to do with Schweitzer's outspoken "modern" ideas on Christianity. The people in authority in the

Paris Missionary Society were afraid that his missionary teachings might not be good for the Africans! Schweitzer was asked to come before the Committee of the Society to be examined about his beliefs so that it might decide whether he was a fit person. He refused and sent a typical message to the Committee. He said that if the teaching of Christ, "He that is not against us is for us," be agreed, then the Committee should accept even a Mahommedan if he offered to go and cure sick people. Anyway, just to please them, Schweitzer promised that he would only practice medicine. On other matters he would be "as silent as a carp." His offer was accepted.

Only one obstacle remained. Dr. Schweitzer was a German doctor with a degree from a German University. The French Government must give him the necessary permission to practice in French territory. Good and influential friends helped him in this matter and so, at last, the time had come when he could start to make good that promise, given when he was twenty-one at Gunsbach. Only now he was not alone. His wife, Helene, was at his side—ready to share his work and support him in all he did.

From Gunsbach to Lambaréné

It is a long way from Gunsbach in Alsace to Lambaréné in
Equatorial Africa. Traveling is not just a matter of covering
distances. It is quite possible to cover thousands of miles and
still arrive in places very much like those we left. Such was
certainly not the case for Dr. Schweitzer and his wife. On
Good Friday, 1913, they set out by train on a journey which
was to end in a dugout canoe, paddled by a crew of Negroes

on a tropical river. They traveled over land and sea for over three weeks but, when you compare their starting and finishing places, it is no exaggeration to say that they traveled backwards through several hundreds of years. They left a civilized, healthy and cultivated land. They arrived in a primitive, fever- and disease-ridden, savage jungle. Let us look for a moment at the sort of place that was French Equatorial Africa in 1913, in order to understand a little of the self-denying heroism of Dr. and Mrs. Schweitzer.

The River Ogowe flows into the Atlantic Ocean on the west coast of Africa, just to the south of the big bulge. It is a big river—over a mile wide in places. Two hundred miles upriver, on the banks of a tributary, stands Lambaréné—just forty miles south of the Equator. Naturally, it is very hot. The average temperature, all the year round, is about 80°F. and the nights are nearly as hot as the days. Heat of this sort is bearable when the climate is dry. On the banks of the Ogowe it is very humid. Some sixty inches of rain fall in an average year and, although there are dry seasons and rainy seasons, much of the low-lying land along the river is a steamy swamp. Vegetation grows vigorously. Great trees, like the the mahogany and okoume, dominate the landscape of the dark, unknown forest. The river has no definite banks. The mud stretches into the trees. The undergrowth is thick and luxuriant and enormous creepers entwine the trees and scramble everywhere. Dead and rotting vegetation is soon submerged in the living forest.

Where the land is cultivated it suits such crops as coffee,

cocoa, pepper and other spices. Neither corn nor potatoes can be grown because it is too warm and moist: the potatoes make enormous stalks but grow no tubers and the grain grows very tall but produces no ears. Cattle cannot be kept because the grass does not suit them and, in any case, the tsetse fly would kill them, for it carries the germs of sleeping sickness.

In the forest are many kinds of birds, monkeys, gorillas, and enormous numbers of snakes, many of them deadly. In the rivers are hippopotamuses, crocodiles and fishes of many kinds. The electric eel, which can kill a person, occurs quite frequently. Larger animals, such as leopards, antelopes and elephants are found where the forest is not so dense. Insects abound. Great spiders, beetles, gorgeous butterflies, flies and the dreaded mosquito, which infects people with malaria and other diseases, all abound.

Most of the peoples who live in these regions are pure Negroes. They belong to different tribes and some of them were cannibals. For many years these primitive, unfortunate people were preyed upon by white men who captured them and, with unspeakable cruelty, carried them off across the Atlantic to slavery. When the slave trade was finally stamped out the white man introduced the curse of alcohol. The natives were paid for their timber with crude spirits and thousands more died. Their way of living was very primitive. When they became ill from one of the host of diseases found in their country, including leprosy, they were "treated" by their witch doctors. More often than not they died slow, painful deaths.

When the French took over the administration things began to improve. Missionaries came and, in 1860, some American Presbyterians established themselves along the River Ogowe. They had a hard time. The natives, remembering the slave traders, naturally mistrusted them. In addition, this was a very unhealthy country for white people. After two or three years of this climate the white man must go back to a cooler climate to recover his strength or he will die.

This was the place in which Albert Schweitzer chose to go and live and work. The Americans left in 1892 and the Paris Missionary Society took over. It had four Mission Stations along the River Ogowe and there were three more run by the Roman Catholics. There had been no doctor in Lambaréné for many years when Albert Schweitzer arrived. There was no hospital either—just land where one might be built.

The last part of the Schweitzers' journey commenced when the little river steamer *Alembe* reached the village of Lambaréné. There was no one to meet them. As they wondered how they would get themselves and all their luggage to the Mission Station, an hour's journey distant by canoe, they saw two native dugouts come dashing up to the ship. These dugout canoes are simply made by hollowing out a tree trunk and shaping the ends roughly to points. They are long and narrow, not very comfortable and, seemingly, not very safe either. The Schweitzers didn't think so, anyway, but as they went on and were not overturned they began to have more confidence in the native boys who paddled them. Paddling is done standing up and the crew keep time with one another by singing a monotonous chant, "Yah-nya, yah-nya, yah-nya —neeeeeeen-yah!" or else, "Tzeh, poba-hoba, tzeh, tzut-tzut!"

As the evening sun lit up the river, the canoe turned into a side stream and the Schweitzers saw for the first time the Mission Station which was to be their home. A small cluster of white buildings on a small hill, the river down below and the impenetrable forest all around—that was Lambaréné in 1913. In this little community the Schweitzers were welcomed by the few white folks and the many Negroes and then, as darkness fell—which it does very suddenly at about six o'clock—Dr. and Mrs. Schweitzer were shown to their little bungalow. It was very small—a four-roomed place, built on iron posts about two feet above the ground, and the children had decorated it with flowers and greenery ready for the new doctor.

Before going to supper with some of the Mission staff, Dr. Schweitzer tells of how he sat outside his bungalow and listened, in the dark, to the African children singing an evening hymn in the schoolroom. His journey had ended, these were the people he had come to help; we can understand him when he says that he felt deeply moved at that moment.

After supper the children came and stood outside the veranda of the bungalow and sang a song of welcome. We can imagine how tired the Schweitzers must have been and how glad they were to settle in their new, little home. But before they could sleep—just to remind them that this was Africa, not Alsace—there was a battle to wage with big spiders, flying beetles and other insects!

At six o'clock next morning the Mission Station bell rang to mark the start of a new day—Dr. Schweitzer's first day in his new medical practice. The news that the doctor had "hung up his shingle," so to speak, had traveled far and wide and from the very beginning a steady stream of sick and suffering natives came to Lambaréné. Here was Dr. Schweitzer's first problem. The people had been told not to bother the doctor, except for very serious cases, for three weeks after he arrived. The reason was because all the medical stores—drugs, bandages and instruments—were coming upriver by the next boat. There had been no room for the big packing cases aboard the *Alembe*. The people ignored these instructions, however. All they knew was that they were sick and, at Lambaréné, was a new medicine man who could take away their sickness. They did not understand the science of medicine so they called Dr. Schweitzer "Oganga," which means witch doctor. They thought that he, like their own medicine men, cured illness and pain by witchcraft. They also believed that, just as he could take away illness, so he could also cause it. They believed in the evil eye, by means of which they thought Dr. Schweitzer, like their own witch doctors, could give some illness or complaint to a person a great distance away. However, they bore him no grudge for that. So long as they could come to him for help and relief from pain, then all was well.

Until the next steamer arrived, Dr. Schweitzer had a difficult time. He had brought only a few items of medicine and dressings in his luggage, he had as yet no hospital nor surgery, and more and more sick and suffering people were arriving. Moreover, he did not know their language. Long before he arrived arrangements had been made for a Negro teacher from another Mission further up the Ogowe to come and act as interpreter and assistant. But N'Zeng didn't turn up when he was wanted and although the doctor sent messages to him, it was in vain. N'Zeng was involved in a long dispute over some property in his village, so Dr. Schweitzer had to manage without him. Of course he did manage—none of the sick people were turned away.

Chicken-House Clinic

A very welcome sound was heard at Lambaréné Mission
on the night of April 26th, 1913. It was the whistle of the
river steamer and it meant that the hospital supplies— and
the special piano which the Paris Bach Society had presented
to Dr. Schweitzer—had arrived. The captain of the steamer
would not risk bringing his ship up the side stream which led
to the Mission Station, so all the big cases were unloaded at

the Roman Catholic Mission on the Ogowe. The problem was how to get seventy packing cases and the piano transported by dugout canoe. A full-sized upright piano, with pedals attached to make it resemble an organ, in a zinc-lined packing case to protect it from insects and damp, seemed an impossible cargo for a hollowed-out tree trunk. However, there was one canoe, made from an enormous tree, which could carry a load of three tons. It took the piano with the greatest of ease.

For three days all hands at the Mission Station were hard at work bringing the heavy cases from the river up the hill to the bungalow—and the doctor worked as hard as anybody. At last it was all done and then there was a new problem. Where on earth could all the things be stored ready for use? Dr. Schweitzer had been promised a small timber-frame, corrugated-metal building for his hospital, but there was no one to build it. The people of the River Ogowe were chiefly employed in the timber trade—cutting down huge trees and floating the logs down to the sea, where they were shipped to Europe. In 1913 the timber trade was flourishing and there was good money to be made, so the people had no time for building hospitals.

Dr. Schweitzer did the best he could by having shelves put up in his bungalow, but he could not do medical work there. It would not have been safe to bring people with all sorts of diseases—many of them infectious—into his house. Patients had to be treated and have their wounds dressed outside, and that was very trying work in the hot sun. Dr.

Schweitzer looked around for some place where he could work under cover and sheltered from the frequent tropical rainstorms. The only place was an old chicken house, which had been built by a former missionary. It was better than nothing. The Schweitzers scraped the walls and floor clean, whitewashed them and turned the place into a little, one-bed hospital—an old camp bed! It was stifling inside, the roof was full of holes so that Dr. Schweitzer had to wear his sun helmet all day—but it was a start!

Dr. Schweitzer worked a long day in his little, chickenhouse clinic. He started at 8:30 a.m. and worked until 6 p.m., with an hour and a half for lunch. Fortunately he soon found a good interpreter and assistant, a Negro of the Galoan tribe called Joseph. Joseph worked as a cook for white people and spoke French very well—except that he *would* use butcher's terms for the human body! He would tell the doctor that a patient had a pain in his leg-of-mutton, or that another had trouble in her loin chops! Still, the doctor understood, and set about curing the pains.

It would have been impossible to record all the patients' names so each one was given a little cardboard disc with a number on it. Most of the patients regarded the little disc as something magic, hung them round their necks and never lost them. When they came back, Dr. Schweitzer only had to look up the number in his book to find all details of the case and so could continue the treatment. That part of the system worked pretty well but there was always trouble over medicine bottles. In such a hot, humid climate medicines and ointments could only be issued to patients in well-corked bottles or in tin boxes. Cardboard boxes were quite useless. Despite the strictest instructions that they must be returned, the black patients liked to keep their bottles and tins. Dr. Schweitzer saw his work being seriously hampered by shortage of bottles so he kept writing to his friends in Europe, asking for bottles, tins and similar containers.

Another difficulty concerned the instructions about taking medicines. Dr. Schweitzer could never be sure that patients would not swallow all the medicine at one go, eat the ointment which was for rubbing on their skins or rub on the powders they were meant to take! It was important, for reasons of prestige as well as those of health, that people should get better after taking medicines. They had confidence in the white man's skill and Dr. Schweitzer was anxious not to lose it. Some of his earliest successes were in the treatment of a terribly irritating skin disease called scabies. Many of the natives suffered agonies with it and their bodies were torn and bleeding with scratching. Dr. Schweitzer's ointment for treating scabies was a mixture of sulphur, crude palm oil, oil from sardine tins and soft soap! It worked magnificently. Three applications and the scabies were gone. Schweitzer's Scabies Ointment (maybe they called it that in their own language) became famous among the natives.

And so, in the suffocating little chicken house with the broken roof, Dr. Schweitzer commenced his noble self-sacrificing work. There was no shortage of patients for, as one African said to the doctor, "Here among us everyone is sick."

Perhaps it was that statement which made Schweitzer compare Europeans and Africans with Dives and Lazarus of the parable told by Christ. Like Dives, the Europeans are rich compared with the Africans—richer by far in such things as medical science and skill and the wherewithal to heal sick people. The parable goes on to describe Lazarus as "the beggar which laid at the rich man's gate." In the parable Dives chose to ignore the need of poor Lazarus. Schweitzer determined that the white man should not treat the Africans in the same manner.

Try for one moment to compare the operating theater in a modern hospital—the spotless cleaniness, the perfect lighting, magnificent equipment and gleaming instruments, the surgeons, anesthetists and nurses—with that in a tiny, dilapidated chicken house on the banks of a tropical river. There is no lighting or ventilation, the roof leaks, every medicine or surgical dressing has to be brought from another building because there is no room, the heat and dampness make it almost impossible to keep instruments clean and sharp. How could any man practice surgery under these conditions? Dr. Schweitzer did his level best but there were things he couldn't do, patients he couldn't save. We can imagine him saying, again and again during those first months at Lambaréné, "Oh! if only I had a real hospital."

Not much could be done until some native labor became available but, in the meantime, Dr. Schweitzer looked round the little clearing in the forest to see where he could best place his hospital. He decided on some ground at the foot of the little hill where his bungalow stood—not far from the river. In July he went to a conference of all the missionaries working on the River Ogowe, held at Samkita, thirty-five miles upriver. The journey was quite exciting. The canoe had no sooner got into the main river, after an early morning start, than the crew saw some black shapes moving in the water. They were hippopotamuses! The hippopotamus is a nasty creature to meet when it is swimming near your canoe because, on the very slightest provocation, it will attack or, worse still, come up underneath the boat and upset everyone. In a river where crocodiles and electric eels live, that is not particularly to be desired!

The conference decided that Dr. Schweitzer must have a hospital building, it agreed on the spot he had chosen and it voted him 4,000 francs (about $400.00 in 1913) to help build it. The homeward journey from Samkita was a happy one. Now something could be done! No time was lost and, with Dr. Schweitzer himself taking a spade to help, eight native timber workers, who were loaned to the Mission, started on leveling the site.

Once the site was cleared, building began—but it was a slow job because Dr. Schweitzer had to do most of the work himself, together with his now invaluable assistant Joseph and some occasional help from the white people at the Mission. By early November it was nearing completion. The floor was concrete, the walls of corrugated metal, large windows reached to the roof but contained no glass. It was cooler to make them of fine wire netting so that the mosquitoes were kept out and the air came in. There were two 13-ft. square rooms—one an operating theater, the other a consulting room, and two small rooms, a dispensary and a sterilizing room. One of the greatest assets for the doctor was the shelving all around the rooms. Now there was a place for all his drugs and equipment!

Outside the hospital were two other buildings—constructed in native style of upright posts and roofs made of leaves— which were to be the patients' waiting room and the hospital "ward." In the open shed which was the ward Dr. Schweitzer marked out on the ground where each "bed" was to go and then he set some of the relatives of patients to work to construct them. They went off into the forest with axes and by that night all the beds, such as they were, were ready. Four short posts, with V-shaped tops into which the long, side pieces fitted and were lashed. Two short end-pieces and then a "mattress" made of creeper stalks woven together. On top, to make it more comfortable, was heaped dried grass—and that was a hospital bed!

But before all this was ready Dr. Schweitzer had to perform his first major operation. It was on a native named Ainda, who had a most serious rupture, known as a strangulated hernia. Ainda had seen other people with this and he had seen them die fairly soon afterwards in great agony. He begged the white doctor to operate and save him. One of the schoolroom bedrooms was hastily turned into an operating room. Mrs. Schweitzer gave the anesthetic and one of the missionaries acted as assistant and handed to Dr. Schweitzer the instruments as he needed them. It must have been a matter of considerable anxiety. This is a big operation even in a properly equipped hospital. Could it be successfully performed under these conditions? Happily, everything went well. The operation was a complete success and the patient recovered. Ainda, who had amazed Dr. Schweitzer by his trustfulness (he even climbed on to the operating table himself), lived when, but for Dr. Schweitzer, he would have died. How satisfied the doctor must have been! Ainda was satisfied, too. He wanted to pay for what he thought was the beautiful thread with which his wound had been sewed up.

Not all the doctor's cases were as straightforward. There were those with diseased minds as well as the physically sick. Some of the insanity was of an extremely dangerous type, moreover—lunatics who sometimes committed murder during their madness. The natives dealt with such people in very cruel fashion. They were tied hand and foot, often so that the ropes bit deeply and drew blood. One night Dr. Schweitzer was called from his bed for what seemed an urgent case. He went and found a woman tied to a palm tree with all her family seated on the ground in front of her, staring at her. The old lady had become insane. Dr. Schweitzer told the people to untie her but only after some persuasion would they do so. Immediately she was free the woman rushed at the doctor and tried to smash the lantern he carried. The relatives ran shrieking for their lives. Dr. Schweitzer quietly seized the woman by the hand and told her to sit down, which she did. He then gave her an injection of morphia and, in a short time, she was sleeping peacefully. In a few days she was better of her temporary madness. The people were amazed. The doctor, they said, was a great magician. He could even cure madness!

Most people in Europe have heard of sunstroke and perhaps some have had the experience of being sick for a day or two after being in the sun. When Dr. Schweitzer first arrived in Africa he was told that the sun is one's greatest enemy. He was most careful never to go out without his sun helmet and always to protect the back of his neck. He often had white patients in his hospital with bad sunstroke, which could even be fatal. A man who was tipped out of his canoe lost his helmet in the water. Although he lay flat in the boat as soon as he got back and covered his head with his coat, it was too late and he was very ill. The native people do not, of course, suffer from sunstroke.

Many amazing cases were brought to Dr. Schweitzer. There was the little boy with a piece of broken bone sticking four inches out from his leg and festering so badly that no one would come near him. Dr. Schweitzer operated on his leg and then restored the boy, who was little more than a skeleton, to health. Soon he became fat and could walk again. On the other hand, there was the young man who was terribly mauled by a hippopotamus. Unfortunately he was brought to hospital while the doctor was attending to some sick people twenty miles away. Joseph did his best for the poor man until the doctor returned. The only chance was an amputation but it was too late and the man died. Then a strange thing happened. His relatives claimed that he died due to the fault of another young man who was in the canoe with him. They might have killed him if Dr. Schweitzer had not intervened and kept the unfortunate man at the Mission Station! On another day there was a pathetic arrival at the hospital. An old man and woman, scarcely able to stand from exhaustion and hunger, arrived after a canoe journey of 250 miles upstream, for the doctor's fame had spread even that far. The old man had leprosy and, at that time, there was no known cure. Nevertheless, they were not turned away. The white doctor did what he could, even for the hopeless cases.

Not very long after building the first hospital another building was needed—but it had to be erected across the river, away from the others. It was needed for people suffering from one of the most widespread of all diseases along the Ogowe River—the dreaded sleeping sickness. It is deadly and sometimes as many as one in every three persons dies with it. It is a difficult disease to diagnose and it takes a long time to kill—but kill it does in the end. Insects, especially the tsetse fly and the mosquito, carry it. The tiny germ of sleeping sickness is only about one five-hundred-thousandth of an inch long and, to establish the presence of the disease, Dr. Schweitzer had to put a drop of the patient's blood under the microscope—and, even then there might be no germ in that drop! It might take hours to diagnose this disease—and all the time there were dozens of other patients, all with ailments, waiting to be treated. To cure sleeping sickness it was essential to give injections while the germ was still in the blood. Once it got into the brain or spine, little could be done.

Other sufferings of these poor people came from sores and ulcers—some of them terrible and revolting—and from various parasites, such as the little sandfly which gets under the toe-nail and leaves a little lump. Cutting out this lump often left a septic wound and, maybe, meant cutting off the toe. Dr. Schweitzer remarked that in 1913 there were very few natives who had ten complete toes. Only long patient work could cure some of these ills but the happiness of those who were cured was a grand reward.

We finish this chronicle of ills which Dr. Schweitzer and his wife had to fight by telling the story of a hernia patient. For hundreds of miles he had come, suffering untold agonies and soon to die unless he could get to the doctor in time. Quickly he was brought to Dr. Schweitzer who quietly told him not to fear. He would be put to sleep, the doctor said, and when he woke there would be no more pain. Trustingly the man went into the operating theater, the operation was performed, with Joseph and Mrs. Schweitzer doing their parts—the latter giving the anesthetic and Joseph acting as surgeon's assistant. Some hours later the doctor sat by the patient's bed, waiting for him to recover consciousness. (The natives believed that Dr. Schweitzer "killed" them, performed the operation and then brought them to life again!) The African opened his eyes, looked round and saw the doctor.

"I've no more pain! I've no more pain!" he said. What a wonderful scene!

Stupidity of War

In the summer of 1914 Dr. Schweitzer went down to the coast. He was suffering from a painful abscess and he considered that the doctor at Cape Lopez should operate on it. Luckily, it burst of its own accord and so, when he got over the first discomforts, he and his wife were able to enjoy a few days of rest and sea breezes. That was a wonderful treat after the oppressive heat of Lambaréné. No doubt the doctor also enjoyed reflecting on his previous year's work. In the first nine months, before he had his hospital, he had treated over 2,000 patients. He was doing the work he wanted to do—he was relieving pain, healing the sick, telling these poor, primitive people about how the white men, because they had a religion which bade them help other people, were concerned for their brothers. These were happy and comforting thoughts for the Schweitzers—but there was a cloud on their horizon. Back in Europe in the summer of 1914 war was foreshadowed. Schweitzer had even realized this a year previously. He understood the uneasy relations between the two countries he knew best—France and Germany. Because of this, he took the money he needed in Africa in gold, rather than bank notes, and when his wife asked why they burdened themselves with the extra weight, he told her that, if war came, bank notes would lose their value but gold would always buy what they needed.

So it was with forebodings that the Schweitzers went back upriver at the end of July. If war did come in Europe, how would the work of the hospital be affected? Unfortunately, they soon knew. Two days after Dr. Schweitzer got back to Lambaréné he wanted to send a package of medicine down to the coast for a sick lady. Joseph went to the store where the steamer called but he came back without sending his package. The war had started, the steamer was to be taken over by the Government and nobody knew when she would go to the coast again.

For weeks the situation changed very little. There was no

news from Europe and everyone felt cut off, but then came the first effect of the war—one of the most fantastically stupid decisions ever made by Government officials. Because Equatorial Africa was French and because Dr. Schweitzer was born and bred in Alsace, which was then German, he must be treated as an enemy alien! He was confined to his house at Lambaréné, was considered as being under arrest and had to cease work at the hospital. Truly, wars are a form of madness and when nations go to war they behave in what can only be called the ways of insanity!

It is easy enough to understand the reactions of the native people to this example of official foolishness. These white men in Europe, who cared so much for the Negroes, were now engaged in killing one another with greatest ferocity. Well, if that was the way they felt about things, it was their affair— but to prevent the white doctor from continuing his work of mercy and healing and to keep him in his house, doing nothing, that surely was the most ridiculous thing of all! There were still the victims of sleeping sickness, still the lepers, still the children lamed by dreadful sores and ulcers, still the men dying in agony from hernia. The doctor and his hospital were still there, but they must do nothing. No wonder the faith and respect which the men of the primitive forest had for the white races was shaken!

The Schweitzers suffered this indignity with patience and nobility. The doctor turned to his music and his books. He began the preliminary work on his greatest book *The Philosophy of Civilization,* and he helped the other missionaries as far as he was allowed. When Christmas 1914 came, the Schweitzers celebrated it quietly. A little palm tree was their Christmas tree and it was decorated with candles. The Negro children loved the pretty lights and listened to the Christmas story from their friend the doctor but, when the candles were only half burned, the doctor blew them out and took them off the tree. His wife did not understand till he told her gravely that he feared the war would last for at least another year and they would want the Christmas candles twelve months hence. How right he was!

Dr. Schweitzer was again receiving mail and papers from Europe but it was difficult to hide the papers and magazines from the natives. He did not want them to see the pictures of the war—because, quite naturally, he felt rather ashamed of being a white man at that time. One of the Pahouins, a tribe which was once cannibal, asked the doctor if the white men ate one another. Indignantly the doctor said that they did not. "So it is only out of cruelty to one another that they kill?" said the Pahouin!

But better times came. In Paris Dr. Schweitzer's old friend and teacher, the great musician, Widor, heard about the ridiculous state of affairs at Lambaréné. He protested violently to the Government and, gradually, the restrictions on Dr. Schweitzer were relaxed. He was allowed to resume his work in the hospital.

Working at Lambaréné during the war years had its compensations—the feeling that in a world gone mad for slaughter, there was still an opportunity for saving life. But there were difficulties, chiefly of shortages. Supplies from Europe were cut off so medical supplies had to be used with great care. There was also the risk of famine. Two of the chief foods of the people were bananas and manioc. Manioc is what we call, in its refined form, tapioca. The bananas, cooked while still green and eaten with palm oil, were brought from up the river. In 1915, however, elephants extensively damaged the banana plantations so that the fruit became scarce. In normal times the hospital imported rice to make up such shortages in locally grown foods but, during the war, there was no rice. Dr. Schweitzer had to insist that patients brought some of their own food, or that they paid for their treatment with sticks of manioc (which they didn't always do). Only in this way could the risk of starvation be kept off.

Another frequent trouble, which threatened food and medical supplies alike, was the insect peril, and worst of all were the traveler ants. These ants march in close columns of countless millions, eating and destroying everything in their path. Nothing escapes them. One night the Schweitzers heard noises of terror from their chickens. There was no time to lose. Three blasts on a bugle was the alarm signal and everyone rushed to rescue the chickens. In a very short time the ants would have suffocated and killed them—and eaten them, leaving only bare, clean bones. The ants, although not very big, have strong nippers and can give nasty bites. The only thing which deters them is lysol. A few buckets were filled with water mixed with this chemical and sprinkled round the house. The ants went off in another direction and the chickens were saved!

During 1916 Joseph left Dr. Schweitzer. The war was to blame. Shortage of money meant halving his wages, and there was plenty of other work so one cannot wonder that Joseph went elsewhere. A young man named N'Kendju became chief assistant to the doctor—the same one who was rescued from the relatives of the other youth killed by the hippopotamus. Although he did his best, N'Kendju was not such a good assistant as Joseph. This meant more work for the doctor, who was beginning to feel the effects of over three years in that unhealthy climate. Tropical anemia is one result —a disease which makes people very tired after very little exertion. Decayed teeth are another trouble and, as Dr. Schweitzer said, there can be few worse things than bad toothache when you are alone in the African forest. He and his wife became each other's dentists and filled one another's teeth, but the doctor had two which could not be saved. He had to endure the pain because there was no one who could extract them.

In the midst of all this Schweitzer had one great comfort and solace—his special piano and Bach's music. Many were the nights when, with the noises of the jungle outside—insects, frogs, wild beasts—and the noises of the drums along the river there mingled the strains of some of the music of the old German composer. Schweitzer found an understanding of the meaning behind the music of Bach which he never had before.

Still the war went on in Europe. Still the senseless slaughter. Still the natives' puzzlement at the behavior of the white races. The official news was sent round by the District Commissioner for the white people to read. There seemed no hope of any ending; and then, in September 1917, came the crowning stupidity from French officials. Dr. and Mrs. Schweitzer were ordered to pack up and go back to France as prisoners of war! Everything was packed—instruments, drugs, medicines (for now there would be no one to administer them) and then, two days before embarkation, when everything was nailed up in packing cases, a canoe arrived with a man who had a strangulated hernia. Immediately Schweitzer had everything unpacked, the operating theater made ready and the poor man's life was saved. Two days later and there would have been no help for him—as indeed there was not for nearly seven years.

There was a scene of sad farewells when the river steamer left with the Schweitzers. "Oganga," the white doctor, was leaving his people. It was a time of great sorrow, for who knew when he would come back, as he had promised he would? Just as the boat was due to leave, the Roman Catholic Father Superior pushed his way on board, ignoring the protests of the soldiers guarding their "prisoners" and shook hands with Dr. Schweitzer.

"You shall not leave this country," he said, "without my thanks for all the good you have done." It was a fine gesture. The Schweitzers never saw him again. He was dead when they came back.

All along their journey the Schweitzers received kindness. Down at the coast a man sneaked up to the doctor and offered him money, in case he had none. The steward who looked after the Schweitzers on the voyage did what he could to make them comfortable—even though a soldier was put in charge of them to see that they did not speak to anyone on board. The steward did this, not because he expected a tip, but because he had heard of "the doctor from Lambaréné" and what a good man he was. To relieve the tedium of the voyage Schweitzer turned to his music and learned some Bach and Widor compositions by heart.

Eventually the ship arrived at Bordeaux. The Schweitzers were immediately clapped into an old army barracks. Two days afterwards Dr. Schweitzer went down with dysentery. Luckily he had some drugs with him and was able to treat himself, but the aftereffects remained with him for a long time. Three weeks later, in the middle of the night, Dr. and Mrs. Schweitzer were moved to a big internment camp in Garaison in the Pyrenees. This place had once been a monastery, but it was disused for a long time until the war came, and it became an internment camp for aliens. It was a grim, bleak place but the Schweitzers soon found among the other prisoners that there were many who knew them and were kind to them. Schweitzer had cured one man's wife when she fell ill in a prisoner-of-war camp in Africa. He was also recognized by the members of a Gypsy Orchestra, who were interned, and they invited him, as a musician, to their concerts. Soon the Camp Commandant, who was a very just and kindly man, relaxed his order and Dr. Schweitzer was allowed to do medical work among the other prisoners. Garaison was a sad, cold place but the mountain air improved Mrs. Schweitzer's health and it was with regret that the Schweitzers heard, in the spring of 1918, that they were to be moved.

The new internment camp was at St. Remy de Provence, in southeast France and was solely for Alsatians. An unattractive place, it had once been an asylum. Here, for a while, Dr. Schweitzer was allowed to assist the pastor and he often preached sermons, as he had done in the old days at Strassburg. Then the camp doctor moved away so, once more, he worked at his calling of healing the sick. But St. Remy did not agree with the Schweitzers. Both of them became ill and weak so that in July, when they were told that they were to be sent back home to Gunsbach they could not even manage to carry their little bit of luggage to the train. A poor cripple, who was also going back to Alsace, came to help them for he had no luggage of his own.

The journey through Switzerland was cheered by a meeting with the Professor of Theology of Zurich University and a well-known musician. They had heard that the famous Dr. Schweitzer was passing through their city and they came to greet him. Eventually the train reached Strassburg, but it was a different city from that which the Schweitzers had left in 1913. Now all was dark for fear of air raids and no one was on the streets at night.

Turning Point

Schweitzer, sick, tired and sad, now wanted only to get back to his native Gunsbach. He felt that the air of the mountains and the joy of being among his own people would make him well again. It was not easy to get to Gunsbach. It was in the fighting line and no trains ran beyond Colmar. Schweitzer set out alone to walk the ten miles wondering all the time, as the guns roared in the hills and when he saw ruined houses and forests turned into twisted tree stumps by shellfire, what he would find at his journey's end. But Gunsbach still stood. It was battered and the people were in constant peril of shellfire. In the parsonage, which was filled with soldiers, Schweitzer found his father working away, quite unperturbed by the confusions and dangers of war. He learned, to his sorrow, that his mother was dead. She had been knocked down and killed by mounted soldiers two years previously. Father and son settled down together and soon Mrs. Schweitzer joined them.

What an end this was to the great adventure which had started in 1913! Albert Schweitzer was a sick man, his beloved Alsace was torn and ravaged by war, his mother dead and the sick and suffering in Africa were now deserted and dying because there was no one to heal them. What sadness must have filled the mind of Albert Schweitzer in August 1918!

During the last days of August 1918, in stiflingly hot weather, a man and a woman were walking towards the town of Colmar in Alsace. In the distance was the sound of gunfire and all around were the signs and destruction of war. The man obviously was ill. He was dragging himself along the road, helped by his companion, and he frequently had to rest. Eventually, after nearly six agonizing miles, a motor vehicle stopped and gave these two poor people a lift to Colmar. One might have mistaken them for war refugees but, in fact, they were none other than Dr. Schweitzer and his wife. The doctor was a very sick man. He had hoped that his native air in the hills of Gunsbach and the comforts of being at home again after those months in prison camps would have improved his health. But he got steadily weaker and he seemed quite unable to throw off the effects of the dysentery which he had contracted at Bordeaux. As a doctor he knew that the only cure lay in undergoing an operation, so, with no other way of getting to Colmar and thence by train to hospital at Strassburg, he had set out to drag himself wearily and painfully along the road. On September 1st the operation was performed.

As he recovered, Dr. Schweitzer took stock of his position. It was not very encouraging. He had no job and no money. Indeed, he was deeply in debt because he had had to borrow money from the Paris Missionary Society to keep his hospital going during the war years. Some way must be found to discharge these debts. And some way also had to be found to support himself, his wife and the baby which she was expecting. These were not comforting thoughts during a convalescence. But Dr. Schweitzer need not have worried. He had friends in Strassburg and, as soon as he was sufficiently recovered, one of them—the Mayor—offered him a post as doctor at the hospital. He was more than pleased to accept and, no sooner had this happened, than another offer was made. Would he accept the curateship of St. Nicholas's Church, and live in the vacant parsonage? Life seemed to be starting all over again for him and, what is more, the war had ended and Alsace had become French again. Characteristically, Schweitzer remembered the defeated German people. Regularly he walked to the German frontier with a rucksack full of food to send to some of his friends who were starving.

Two happy years followed, although one can be sure that Dr. Schweitzer did not escape the feeling of sadness when he thought of Lambaréné, with no doctor to look after its people. In January 1919, his only child, his daughter Rhena, was born. Another happiness lay in the resumption of his work on his book *The Philosophy of Civilization*. Nor did he forget his music. So, during 1919, we have a picture of a family man, preaching on Sundays, healing in the hospital all the week and working at his books and music in between. But that was not enough. Schweitzer, adept in producing apt descriptive phrases, wrote of this period that he felt rather like a coin which had rolled under a piece of furniture and got lost! He was out of circulation, shut away in that corner of Alsace. He did make one break: he saved every centime he could and went to Barcelona to play the organ at a concert. That appearance gave him confidence. His playing was still good enough to enable him to face the world again.

To do that required courage. During the summer of 1919 a second operation had been found to be necessary and so Dr. Schweitzer was still far from strong. But encouragement came from an unexpected place. The Archbishop of the Swedish Protestant Church sent an invitation to him to come to the University of Uppsala and give a series of lectures. Those lectures marked a turning point. They were a wonderful spiritual experience. Dr. Schweitzer lectured on philosophy and during his last lecture he told of the idea he had formed while in Africa, which he called the Reverence for Life. It was only a continuation of the thoughts he had on that day when, as a boy, his companion wanted him to shoot birds. Life is sacred; Life is something which, once taken, cannot be restored. It was a magnificent lecture on a noble theme.

You may wonder how Dr. Schweitzer lectured to Swedes without knowing their language. He had an interpreter, a young theological student, who translated each sentence to the audience as the doctor uttered it. To lecture in this fashion demands a special technique—one which requires short, distinct sentences. But Dr. Schweitzer knew all about this method. He had used it for years in communicating with the Negroes of Equatorial Africa!

Dr. Schweitzer enjoyed his Swedish trip immensely—the Swedish climate was beneficial to his health and he became very fit once more. Naturally he talked a great deal with his Swedish friends, and thus the Archbishop learned of Schweitzer's worries about his debts. The Archbishop offered a very practical suggestion. The Uppsala University lectures had been well received. Why not extend the idea and deliver lectures to other audiences in Sweden—audiences who would pay to listen? The Archbishop also suggested a series of organ recitals. He felt certain that people would pay good money to hear such a famous organist— and there was plenty of money in Sweden, which was a prosperous country just after the First War. Schweitzer was fired with enthusiasm, especially as the student who translated his speeches offered to travel with him.

During the next three months Schweitzer lectured and played the organ in many places in Sweden. Everywhere he was welcomed and everywhere he delighted his hearers. The tour was a triumphal success and, which was a wonderful encouragement—it paid! He had enough money to pay off some of his biggest debts and he began to hope that he might, after all, return to Lambaréné one day. By a strange twist of fortune those very things which Schweitzer renounced in order to go to Africa were now going to help him to get back there!

The visit to Sweden marked a turning point. Here was a new Schweitzer, active, vigorous, never letting up for a moment. He longed to return to his work at Lambaréné, and set about planning to do so. The next five years were a period of tremendous activity. He was everywhere—Denmark, England, Germany, Spain, Switzerland and Czechoslovakia, lecturing and giving organ recitals. He also wrote an account of his years in Africa, which he called *On the Edge of the Primeval Forest,* for a Swedish publisher. He wrote it in German, and it was translated first into Swedish, and then into English. Later, it sold many thousands of copies in its Danish, Dutch, Finnish and French editions.

All of this meant that he could not continue to work in the hospital at Strassburg, nor act as curate of St. Nicholas's Church. He gave up both posts in 1921 and went to live with his wife and Rhena at Gunsbach again. His father was delighted to have the family with him. In that same year Schweitzer paid a visit to England. He lectured and gave organ recitals at Oxford, Birmingham, Cambridge and London.

There were other books published during this active period, including, in 1923, the first two volumes of *The Philosophy of Civilization*. As he worked on the rest of the book Schweitzer began his preparations for return to Africa. He had made enough money to restart the Lambaréné Hospital and resume the work he had been forced to leave in 1917. The passing days found him busier than ever. The final proofs of his book had to be corrected, the purchases of stores and equipment for the hospital had to be made and, even then, in the midst of all that, he found time to produce yet another book. In some ways that book, the simplest of all the Schweitzer books, is the best. It is called *Memoirs of Childhood and Youth* and it came to be written in a strange manner. Schweitzer was in Zurich on a visit to his friend Dr. Pfister, a psychoanalyist. He wanted to relax so the doctor got him to relate aloud all he could remember about his earliest years. Every word was written down by Dr. Pfister and the result was this charming little book.

There were no difficulties about going back to Lambaréné this time. Dr. Schweitzer was now a Frenchman, for Alsace had become part of France again after the war. Moreover, by every post, there were entreaties for the doctor to return. There was so much work waiting to be done. Disease and sickness still swept along the River Ogowe and the people still died when they might have lived had there only been a doctor available. One great disappointment befell him before his departure, however: Mrs. Schweitzer could not go back with him. She had been unwell for some time and, besides, she now had a small daughter to look after. She knew as well as anyone just what dangers and hardships her husband was going to face in Lambaréné—but she let him go; she even encouraged him. It was a most unselfish decision on her part.

And so, on February 21, 1924, the Dutch cargo boat *Orestes* left the port of Bordeaux bound for West Africa, taking Dr. Schweitzer. He did not travel entirely alone, for he had, as an assistant, a young Englishman from Oxford, a student of chemistry, whose name was Noel Gillespie. Dr. Schweitzer was working up until the moment the boat left and he took aboard four sacks full of unanswered letters! The Customs were suspicious of those sacks. They thought the doctor might be trying to smuggle out some banknotes but, after getting to the bottom of two of the sacks, they gave up and decided that this Dr. Schweitzer must have the biggest fan mail in the world! In fact, many of those letters came from people who had helped, with gifts of money, to make the return to Lambaréné possible. Help had come from France, Switzerland, Sweden, England, Denmark and Czechoslovakia among other countries—and the doctor meant to send replies to all of those letters before he got to the end of his journey! The journey took nine weeks so he probably managed it.

At Douala, in the Cameroons, Dr. Schweitzer and Noel Gillespie left the Dutch ship and boarded the mail boat *Europe,* which took them to the mouth of the Ogowe. They had barely arrived before some of the native people recognized the doctor. What a wonderful reception they gave him! "The doctor is back!" The news traveled like wildfire. Everyone was overjoyed, and we can imagine how the news traveled up the Ogowe and reached Lambaréné long before the old *Alembe*—now an extremely dirty, disreputable, old steamer.

To Dr. Schweitzer little had changed as the *Alembe* steamed up the River Ogowe. On both sides there was still the virgin forest, full of wild animals, silent, impenetrable. This part of Africa was still as poor as ever, largely because its chief product was still timber. All the while there were great trees to fell and then float down the river no efforts at cultivation were worthwhile. The natives could make enough money from the felling to buy food and thus had no need to grow their own. Rice and dried fish, still imported to feed the laborers were the chief foods, because the manioc and bananas were insufficient.

During the last miles on the *Alembe* the doctor's thoughts often dwelt on Lambaréné. What would he find when he reached there? He knew, of course, that the Mission was still there, but what about his hospital? Nearly seven years had passed since he had last seen them, and the jungle can obliterate most things in far less than that time. Once again the steamer reached the landing stage at Lambaréné and the doctor, his companion and all their luggage and stores went ashore. It was some time before the canoes from the Mission Station arrived and, even then, there were not enough of them to transport everything and others had to be hired. Finally all was ready, and as they traveled up the side stream Dr. Schweitzer's eyes were fixed ahead. At last the Mission Station came into sight and, at midday on Easter Saturday, the doctor returned to Lambaréné.

He walked across to where his hospital once stood. What a change! The forest had advanced and almost engulfed everything! What were previously small saplings were now great trees and a smothering undergrowth ran everywhere. The patients' wards were completely gone but the corrugated building still stood—that which was formerly the operating theater and consulting room. The dispensary was still there, too, and both these buildings, except for badly leaking roofs, could be used again. The path up to the doctor's house (which was ready for him once again) had become quite overgrown for no one had walked that way for years. The Mission people told Dr. Schweitzer that they would soon have all the grass cut down so that he might walk in comfort again, but he would not let them. "Let me tread down a path again, as I did before," he said.

Immediately after his midday meal Dr. Schweitzer made a start on getting his hospital ready again. The first job was roof mending, so he set off in a canoe with Gillespie to the native village to get some raffia roof tiles, such as were made by the natives. But there were none to be had. The people in the village no longer made roof tiles and indeed their own roofs were broken and full of holes. Everyone now worked at timber. Timber and yet more timber was required and the pay was good—so why would anyone bother to stitch roof tiles? Promises and threats alike were no good. When Schweitzer, in desperation, said that he wouldn't treat the sick from that village if they didn't find him some roof tiles, the people only laughed. They knew that the threat would never be carried out. Dr. Schweitzer—Le Grand Docteur, as they now called him to distinguish him from all the other white people (who were the "little doctors")— could never be so unkind.

He did not go empty-handed however. An old man took him behind one of the huts and showed him twenty roof tiles. In one place and another he and Gillespie collected another forty-four and so, in pouring rain and in the dark, they went back to the Mission Station with sixty-four roof tiles—enough to repair the operating theater roof. It was a happy Easter Day for Dr. Schweitzer. He was back at Lambaréné. He was getting ready to start work once more.

Return to Lambaréné

Few men in the world can have worked harder than Dr. Schweitzer did during the next four years. From the time of his return to Lambaréné there was no shortage of patients. Everyone had heard of the great work he had done during his previous stay and the cures he had wrought. Many of the people whose lives he had saved were still alive and healthy. Is it any wonder that the sick and suffering from up and down the River Ogowe flocked to the Mission at Lambaréné to be helped and cured? Even if there had been a fully equipped hospital ready to receive them, Dr. Schweitzer would have been a busy man. But there was practically nothing—only two small buildings with the jungle growing all round them. So, for the next years, Schweitzer had to be both doctor and builder. Now he worked with drugs, bandages and instruments, and then, as he put them down, he picked up ax, saw, plane and rule.

Immediately Easter 1924 was over the work of rebuilding started. It took two weeks to get the consulting room and dispensary into something like working order, and then the patients' ward had to be begun. The great worry was still that of obtaining roof tiles. These were made by the natives by binding raffia leaves on a bamboo frame but, as already explained, the people were far too busy making money by working for the timber merchants. Schweitzer and Gillespie combed the country far and wide for leaf tiles. There was a pressing urgency. It was the rainy season and morning after morning Dr. Schweitzer would go into the building which served as a hospital ward to find patients lying on the floor and soaked through with the rain, which had come through the roof. Two of them died from the chills they got in this way. We can understand the despair which the doctor felt about such unnecessary loss of life.

One of the ways of getting building materials, such as leaf tiles or bamboos, or obtaining help with the building work, was to tell patients that they must pay for their treatment by one of these means. Sometimes relatives of sick persons gave the hospital three or four days' work in return for the help which was given to their sick. But Dr. Schweitzer could not always enforce this. Many a poor mother, bringing her child covered all over with dreadful ulcers, could make no contribution. As one would expect, this made no difference to Le Grand Docteur. The child was cured with the new drug which works marvels in these cases, and which had then just been discovered. In the past it was a slow and, for the child, terrifying business of sticking a needle into its arms to give injections. Now there were pills which could be swallowed easily and which effected certain cures. The one drawback was that the pills were very expensive.

The doctor had other failures in his efforts to obtain some sort of payment for his work. A chief came to him with a badly injured hand, caused by the bursting of a gun. He was a very proud man and, even though he was there to be treated, he never let the white men forget that he was a chief. A number of his relatives came with him so the doctor suggested that while the chief was having his treatment, they might do a little building work. None of them took any notice so Schweitzer told the chief that unless they made a contribution he would do no more dressings to the injured hand. He said (although he knew privately there was no such risk) that he would let it "go bad." The chief thereupon promised to send 500 leaf tiles if treatment were resumed. Dr. Schweitzer never got those leaf tiles—but he still could not bring himself to think badly of that chief!

Two of the most dreadful diseases of these people seemed to have increased since 1917. They were sleeping sickness and leprosy—both fairly hopeless unless caught in their early stages. Patients with the former are perhaps the most troublesome of all because treatment is long, slow and difficult. It consists of giving injections every day for six weeks.

A growing habit of the natives which gave Schweitzer a lot of trouble and expense was that of their dumping old, and often dying, people on him. They would be brought during the night and left on his doorstep, so to speak. One poor old man, almost naked and having not even a blanket to lie on nor a mosquito net to prevent him being bitten, was found one morning. He was tenderly cared for during the remaining weeks of his life. There were other cases like this, for the native medicine men were acute enough to recognize sick people for whom there was no hope—and then they had them dumped on the white doctor! Thus, when the poor sufferer inevitably died, the fault was with the hospital and the white doctor, and sometimes some of the patients left the hospital because of this.

Deaths in the hospital brought another great difficulty. The natives had a superstitious horror of the dead and it was often impossible to get them even to help in digging the grave. When a death occurred in the hospital every able-bodied man made himself scarce by going off fishing or visiting his relatives and so, very often, the result was that the people from the Mission, or even Dr. Schweitzer and Noel Gillespie, had to act as sexton, bearers and mourners. There cannot be many doctors in the world who have had to be grave diggers as well! When these poor people died they were given Christian burial by one of the missionaries. There was, for instance, the poor old woman who was left, dying, at the hospital one night. Her neighbors could not be bothered with her. They even refused to cut some wood to make a fire to keep her warm. Her last days were made warm and comfortable and, when she died and was buried, the school children sang a hymn and one of the missionaries told how, when her own people had thrown her out, the old woman had been cared for by the white men. They had done this because they were following the teaching of their leader, whose name was Jesus. Simple words like these, following actions of kindness, often made their important impression on the people of the Ogowe.

At this time, in addition to Noel Gillespie, Dr. Schweitzer had one good and loyal helper, a native named G'Mba. G'Mba could read and write and he soon became a great help to the doctor, able to act as hospital orderly and not unwilling (which earned the admiration of Dr. Schweitzer) to help with such tasks as burials. But perhaps the chief value of G'Mba was shown at mealtimes. There were always people asking to be fed at the hospital. Some of them were too poor to buy food; with others the stock which they had brought with them in their canoes had given out, and yet others came from places where there was famine. So, every day at noon, rations were dispensed—rice, or bananas, or manioc, and sometimes dried fish. The patients then cooked their own meals. When the doctor was too busy, then G'Mba distributed the food—and he was not so easy to get round as the doctor!

The summer of 1924 marked a number of important stages in the development of Dr. Schweitzer's hospital. In July the steamer coming up from the coast brought over seventy packing cases full of equipment and medicines of all kinds. At the same time there arrived a motor launch for use at the Mission Station. This meant much quicker and more certain transportation, for there was always difficulty in finding enough men for paddling one of the larger canoes. The motor boat was powerful enough to tow canoes when large quantities of stores had to be moved. Much more important, however, was the arrival of the hospital's first white nurse. She was from Strassburg, and it was no time at all before Miss Mathilde Kottmann made her presence felt. The place became tidier, the weekly washing was properly done, beds were efficiently made, the chickens were fed and the eggs collected regularly. For a while there was so much to do in the house that Miss Kottmann didn't have time to work in the hospital—but what a difference her coming made!

But Nurse Mathilde Kottmann was not the only additional helper who came to Lambaréné in 1924. In October, just when Dr. Schweitzer was almost at the end of his strength and felt that he could not go on any longer, a new assistant arrived. He was another doctor, a fellow-student from Strassburg, and it is easy to picture the joy of Schweitzer's wel-

108

come to him. His name was Victor Nessmann and, because he was not very old, the Africans soon christened him "the little doctor." It seemed strange to them that one so young could be a doctor.

Dr. Schweitzer now felt that he could press on with the so badly needed buildings, leaving most of the medical work to Dr. Nessmann, but there were many difficulties. One of them was the weather. Normally, there was a dry season at Lambaréné from May to October but, in 1924, the rain continued throughout this period. It caused many troubles. The natives could not make so many expeditions into the forest for bamboos and timber, food became scarce and nobody's health was very good. Poor Dr. Schweitzer suffered agonies with ulcers on his feet, Nurse Kottmann was far from well and, at the end of the year, Dr. Nessmann had a very bad attack of boils. In addition to these three, there were eight white people as patients and, of course, all the natives at the hospital for Christmas, 1924. It was not a very cheerful time.

It would be impossible to recount all the happenings at the hospital in Lambaréné in a short book. Each day brought its own vicissitudes, its trials and triumphs. Not the least of these were the difficulties which a new type of patient to the hospital brought. In the years before the war most of Dr. Schweitzer's patients belonged to the tribes which normally lived in villages on the banks of the Ogowe. They were fairly easy to deal with and the doctor's various helpers spoke their languages and so it was easy to understand what was wrong and to prescribe the right treatment. But, after the war, the timber trade grew to very great proportions and much of the labor was recruited from tribes which lived far in the interior of Africa. Some of these people were Bendjabis —and Bendjabis were difficult people. First, they had six or seven different languages and none of the hospital staff, native or white, could understand them. Secondly, they were savages in every sense of the word, with a different code of behavior from anyone else. Often they would go away when their treatment was only half finished; they were more than reluctant to help by doing work of any kind at the hospital; and they were great thieves. Few of them could understand that it was necessary for the doctor to operate on them to cure their illnesses and pains. They even believed—until the operation was over and they woke to find their pain gone— that the white men were cannibals.

The year 1925 started gloomily, but there were encouragements on the way. The work Dr. Schweitzer was doing had begun to achieve recognition and more help was on the way.

Another doctor was coming to join the hospital staff and this was more than heartening to the two medical men who were working so unsparingly. The new man was Dr. Mark Lauterberg, who came from Berne, Switzerland. His arrival meant that all operation cases could be dealt with in proper fashion. Until his arrival, although Dr. Schweitzer realized that three mornings each week should be devoted to surgery, it was impossible to carry out such a program. Surgery is exhausting work, even in a modern hospital, with nursing and operation theater staff to wait on the surgeon's every requirement and then be able to look after the patient when the operation is all over. Dr. Schweitzer and Dr. Nessmann had no modern theater and no nursing staff, except Miss Kottmann and a few orderlies. The strain of three mornings of operations in a week would have been quite insupportable— so the news of Dr. Lauterberg's coming was a wonderful encouragement.

The difficulty about where the new doctor was to live had to be overcome. With quite insufficient help, Dr. Schweitzer had been struggling to build a little house for Dr. Nessmann. It was to have had but three rooms but, between work at the hospital, lack of any sort of assistance and his own illness, Dr. Schweitzer had only finished one room in nearly three months. Finally, when the house was ready, Dr. Nessmann could have only one of the rooms because of a sudden influx of several white patients. The other two rooms were turned into wards for them.

There was nothing for it but some more building. Building, building, building—Dr. Schweitzer must often have wondered whether he would ever see the end of it! He had one more piece of land and he determined to erect on it a large, ten-roomed, timber and corrugated-metal building for white patients. A Canadian, who had been nursed through a very serious illness at the hospital, decided to help so he went off with a native crew in a big canoe to get hardwood piles, which were then to be dug into the ground and on which the building framework was to rest. He had to go twenty miles to get them. Each evening the two doctors took spades and dug out the soil to level the site. Then, when everyone felt that a start was being made, the wife of the native carpenter died of sleeping sickness. That meant that her husband, according to the custom of his tribe, would sit in his hut, wearing torn clothes, mourning. This would go on for weeks, during which time he would do no work!

However, even if the building work was subject to such difficulties and delays, there was a pleasant surprise coming. A beautiful motor boat with the charming Swedish name, *Tack sa Mychet* (Many thanks), arrived at the hospital. Some of the people in Sweden who had listened to Dr. Schweitzer's lectures and organ recitals had started collecting money in 1922 to buy him a motor boat. It took them nearly three years to get enough but, at last, they had done it. The boat was magnificent—twenty-eight feet long and five feet wide, able to carry one ton, having a speed of seven-and-a-half miles an hour in still water and completely covered by an awning as a protection against the sun. No longer was there the difficulty of scraping together a native crew when a journey for stores or to attend a sick person had to be made and the Mission boat was not available. In any case, the cost of gas and oil was a good deal less than the cost of hiring men to paddle a dugout.

In February another piece of good fortune came the doctor's way. A white man was brought to the hospital suffering with blackwater fever. He was a Pole, named Rochowiack, and, having seen other people die of this fever, he thought that he had little chance. He was wrong. Dr. Schweitzer saved his life and so, to show his gratitude, he offered to give a hand with the new building. He was a carpenter and joiner by trade so his offer was more than gratefully accepted and the building began to move forward again. Dr. Schweitzer, once more, had to divide his time between the hospital and the building site and, of course, there was also all the work of administration, keeping an eye on supplies, ordering more when they were needed and generally keeping everyone happy and cheerful. What a constitution he must have had to be able to stand it all—and how glad he must have been to welcome Dr. Lauterberg in March 1925!

The new doctor soon made an impression. Dr. Lauterberg was a surgeon, and he had been at Lambaréné for only a very short time before he took his place in the scheme of things. Operations took place on three mornings each week and the natives soon had a name of their own for the new surgeon. It was N'Tschinda-N'Tschinda, which means "The man who cuts boldly." However, N'Tschinda-N'Tschinda had to learn that he must not fully justify his name. There are many operations performed in Europe where the amputation of an arm or leg, or hand or foot, is considered to be the only safe course. But, as Dr. Schweitzer pointed out to his new assistant, that was not a good way of doing things in Africa. Too many amputations would lead to the hospital getting a reputation among the people of being a place where arms and legs were cut off—and that would drive people away instead of attracting them to the hospital. It sometimes meant more complicated surgery—but it was well worth it.

A Difficult Year

As the autumn of 1925 passed on into winter there was no reduction in the activity at Lambaréné. In fact, there was so much work that Joseph, who came back to Dr. Schweitzer during the postwar years, cut short a time of mourning for his brother and returned to work.

He explained his action to Dr. Schweitzer by saying, "The doctor is a slave to his work and Joseph is the doctor's slave."

Dr. Schweitzer had, once again, started building, with the expert help of a young Swiss carpenter. But there were the usual difficulties in getting suitable materials. Strangely, timber was the worst of all. True, it grew everywhere and was exported in huge quantities, but that was in logs. Getting logs sawed into planks or beams was almost an impossibility. For example, a timber merchant gave Dr. Schweitzer thirty fine mahogany beams in return for curing one of his men. The beams were about 10″ square and the measurement required by the doctor was 5″ square. For weeks Dr. Schweitzer tried to get his beams sawed into four but without any success. Then the wife of a timber merchant got a very bad throat and came to the hospital for treatment. In return, her husband loaned the doctor two of his sawyers—and the job was done. The roof could then be put on the building because the beams were in place.

In June Dr. Schweitzer went down to the coast to get a change of air and a little rest. He needed both but, although he may have got the former, he had little rest. Too many people knew that he was there and flocked to him with all sorts of complaints to be cured, and of course, he could not turn them away. Perhaps it was as well that he had plenty to do. Just a few weeks previously he had received the news that, back home in Gunsbach, his father, old Pastor Schweitzer, had died, His work was a comfort to him in this time of sorrow. Schweitzer's father had been interested throughout in his son's wonderful, self-sacrificing career. The father's pride had been equalled by the son's devotion and Albert Schweitzer felt a severe sense of parting when his father died.

Once his little break (it could not be called a holiday) at the coast was over, Schweitzer went back to the hospital to find a situation bordering on crisis. A battle confronted him—perhaps the most serious he ever had to fight, and there were two deadly enemies. They were severe famine, with possible death by starvation for hundreds of people, and one of the most dreadful epidemic diseases—dysentery.

The famine arose from a number of causes. First, the weather. It had rained almost continuously throughout what should have been the dry season. Such crops as the Africans grew could not be planted because the ground was not fit—neither could the annual fishing be done. Normally, large quantities of river fish were caught and then dried over fires and stored. Another cause of famine was the Africans' own improvidence. There was plenty of work at timber—felling trees, trimming the logs and floating them down the river. The money to be earned was good—so nearly every able-bodied man went to work at timber and consequently the growing of food was neglected. At first this didn't worry them too much. Large quantities of rice were imported and this took the place of the bananas and manioc. But rice—especially the polished white rice—does not make a good diet. It contains no vitamins and the result was, when sickness and disease came, the African people had little or no resistance.

The first outbreak of dysentery occurred at a timber camp sixty miles from Lambaréné. Dr. Schweitzer went there with Dr. Nessmann to do what they could. It was a difficult journey —forty-five miles downriver by motor boat and then fifteen miles by canoe up a small, rapidly flowing side stream. Quite a number of cases were treated on the spot but, because there were some who were seriously ill, much as Dr. Schweitzer disliked the idea, they had to be brought back to the hospital. The reason for his reluctance was that no isolation ward existed at Lambaréné, and it was extremely difficult to keep other patients away from the dysentery cases.

Lambaréné Hospital was a stricken spot by July 1925. So many of the patients had dysentery that there was nowhere to put them. Despite every precaution taken by the white people, the natives continued to expose themselves to infection. They could not be made to realize that dysentery germs are found in water, which easily becomes polluted. Dr. Schweitzer found people bringing water from the river, filthy and swarming with germs, to patients in the hospital because it was too much trouble to go to the spring, which was farther away. It all seemed so hopeless.

Those who were ill with dysentery had to be cared for— often a tiring business, for the patient becomes so weak that he is too helpless to take his food and must be fed by hand. Dr. Schweitzer and his devoted helpers had to do this—and all the time there was all the normal work of the hospital— operations, dressings, nursing—and famine and hunger were stalking in the background.

One day, tired and dispirited by difficulties which would have defeated a lesser man, Dr. Schweitzer came across Africans drawing polluted water to give to patients in the hospital. Wearily he stopped them and tried to make them understand. Then he went back to his consulting room, sat in his chair and said, "What a fool I was to come out here to try to help people like these!" Joseph heard and replied, "Yes, Doctor, here on earth you are a great fool—but not in Heaven!" Schweitzer did not altogether appreciate the remark. A bit more practical help in running the hospital meant far more to him than pious phrases! To him Christianity is—as it should be—a practical, real thing. It is in the work we do for our fellow creatures and the help we bring to those who need it far more than in piety, observance of religious practices and so forth.

Fortunately the foresight of Dr. Schweitzer averted the danger of starvation at the hospital. He laid in large stocks of rice and could dole out up to 168 pounds per day to his patients and staff. But rice is a poor substitute for bananas, manioc and fish, and the hospital was full of patients so thin and emaciated from the effects of dysentery and a rice diet that they looked like walking skeletons.

In October, 1925, another white nurse, Emma Hausknecht, a teacher from Alsace and an old friend of Dr. Schweitzer's, arrived. Her job was to keep the hospital clean and properly organized, to take care of and to distribute food, and to superintend all the work in the hospital grounds.

Truly, 1925 was an anxious and difficult year for Dr. Schweitzer but, as is so often the case, it was out of these same anxieties and difficulties that new hopes, new plans and schemes and finally, a magnificent new hospital emerged. The dysentery epidemic made the doctor realize that he must have isolation wards for patients with infectious diseases. He needed more and better buildings for everyone; and he also planned, with great wisdom, gardens and plantations for his hospital so that, never again would there be the risk of famine because the Africans had not cultivated their own plantations. But how was all this to be achieved?

There was no further room for extension on the Mission Station at Lambaréné. All the ground was already covered and the hospital buildings were, in any case, too near the school and houses. Some other site would have to be found. A place was needed, too, for the frequent mental patients who were brought to the doctor. At the Mission Station he had only one small, windowless cell for locking up these poor mad people—and even then he sometimes could not continue to treat them because of the noise they made, which disturbed the other patients. Mental patients could be cured only if there was proper accommodation for them.

Driven on by all these considerations, Dr. Schweitzer began to look round for a suitable site for the sort of hospital he had always wanted—taking care that nobody knew what was in his mind, for he did not want to disappoint anyone. He found a suitable place nearly two miles upstream. Once it had been the site where the old sun king N'Kombe had lived and some big villages had stood there. They had now gone and the place was deserted, but the trees which had grown up were small and could be easily cleared—and there were many oil palms, planted by the former inhabitants, which would be a start for the plantation which Dr. Schweitzer had in mind.

The proceedings for acquiring land usually took a long time, but the Government District Commissioner was helpful. He gave permission for the hospital to acquire the land and get on with its job while the formalities were proceeding.

That night, when Dr. Schweitzer came back from his visit to the District Commissioner, he called a meeting of all the doctors and nurses. They met, wondering what it was all about, and then they heard the news. A new hospital, big enough for every kind of case! New houses for the staff! Proper buildings, roofed with galvanized metal instead of those leaf tiles which were so hard to get! Over 170 acres of land—room to spread, room for gardens and plantations! There were shouts of joy. What wonderful news! Even the Africans caught the spirit. These white people who had been so hard-pressed, so despondent at times, were now happy. They told each other, "It must be great news to have done this!"

Jungle Hospital

Building a hospital large enough to accommodate 200 patients, together with their relatives and friends (who very often had to bring their sick long distances and could not, thus, be turned away) and the medical staff's houses, over 200 miles upriver in Equatorial Africa is the sort of job which would give a big building contractor plenty to think about. Yet Dr. Schweitzer—clergyman, musician, philosopher, physician and surgeon—was ready to tackle it and to add the title of "builder" to his other qualifications. What an amazing man! Without doubt, he was the only person who could get the new hospital built. The Africans, even when famine made it necessary for them to work for their food, were not an industrious people. But then neither should we be in that climate, and on their diet. Probably the only person for whom they would make an effort was "the old Doctor." And so, leaving his two colleagues to run the hospital, Dr. Schweitzer became a building foreman and started the big job.

The first task was to mark out the area and decide where the various huts and hospital wards were to be built. That wasn't easy. Often it meant hacking a way through thick undergrowth, and keeping a constant watch for snakes— some of them deadly poisonous. Another enemy was the red ant. When a nest was disturbed it was a case of running away as fast as possible. These ants would crawl all over you and give the most ferocious bites. Then there were the swampy places. Long poles had to be driven into them so that they could be crossed. It was all a slow, laborious business in that still, steamy heat.

Each morning came the business of rounding up the day's labor gang. Some of the Africans were adept at hiding away until the canoes had left for the new site, others pretended that they were not fit for work. Dr. Schweitzer had to be everywhere for they knew they could not fool him. Even when he got his gang two miles upstream, they took a lot of coaxing to get on with cutting down trees, hacking away

creepers and clearing the ground. Their best working time
of the day was the late afternoon: with the evening meal
getting near as a reward for their work, the men would make
a real onslaught on the forest with axes and knives. And so,
gradually, the site was cleared. Some of the ground was then
immediately dug and corn planted. Dr. Schweitzer wanted
some other food to replace the imported rice, which provided
insufficient nourishment. The only trees which were spared
were the oil palms and the fruit-bearing trees—mangoes and
papayas. Many of them were smothered and almost strangled
by the creepers which enmeshed them. Once the creepers
were cut away, the trees, as if glad to be freed, started to
bear fruit again. This was all a part of Dr. Schweitzer's plan.
He wanted his new hospital to be surrounded by fruit trees
so that everyone could have all the fruit he wanted. Health
would certainly improve as a result.

Dr. Schweitzer was a tired man when he arrived back at
the hospital each evening. It was a rule that all work finished
at dark because of the risk of mosquito bites and the conse-
quent malaria but, while the others rested in their huts and
houses, the "old Doctor" had all his writing to do. There were
drugs and stores to be ordered, letters of thanks to be sent to
all the people in Europe and America who gave money to
help keep the hospital going—and there was the book about
St. Paul. It had been started fourteen years earlier and was
slowly being finished at this rate. Even then, a few short
hours were snatched now and again for playing the beloved
music of Bach on the piano with the pedals attached to make

it resemble an organ. Music often kept Schweitzer going when little else could have done so.

After clearing the site, building began. Everyone agreed that there should be no more huts with leaf-tile roofs. They were far too much trouble. Often, after a morning's work in the surgery and wards, the doctors had to spend the afternoon at roof repairs—afternoons which should have been devoted to the patients. So they decided the new buildings should be of hardwood frames (mahogany and suchlike—which ants do not attack), with corrugated-metal walls. They had to be built up on piles off the ground because of the risk of floods. A special kind of timber was needed for the piles and it grew in only a few places near the river. The nearest was about sixteen miles upstream—so Dr. Nessmann was given the job of felling what was needed and bringing it downstream. That took a long time, and so did their preparation. In order that the piles should not rot, they had to be charred in a fire and then quenched in water. All this had to be superintended, and Dr. Schweitzer reckoned he had done well if he got thirty piles charred in a day.

The first building of the new hospital was planned to be about eighty feet long by sixteen feet wide. Over eighty piles were needed for it alone. What a vast labor Dr. Schweitzer undertook in the building of his new hospital! Hundreds of piles had to be brought from the forest, cut and charred, holes had to be dug and stones put into them, measurements had to be taken (Dr. Schweitzer found that he dared not leave that to a native or mistakes were bound to occur) and levels ascertained. But the work went on. Five months after it started there came a great day for the builder-in-chief. A young carpenter arrived from Switzerland to give a hand. What a relief it was to Dr. Schweitzer to have someone he could rely on to do the job while he was absent!

While Dr. Schweitzer was in the midst of all this new construction, news arrived from Prague that the University there had decided to honor him with the degree of Doctor of Philosophy. I wonder what the University authorities would have thought of their new Doctor of Philosophy if they could have seen him superintending a gang of laborers digging holes and setting up piles in the middle of the equatorial forest!

As if to spur the doctor on with his work, one night a mental patient at the hospital, in a maniacal frenzy, broke out of his small cell and spread terror among the patients. As the cell could not be made strong enough to hold the poor creature there was nothing to do but send him back to his own people. Schweitzer did so with great reluctance and much sadness of heart, for he knew that the poor demented creature would probably spend his time chained to a tree like an animal. The new hospital was to have proper cells for these unfortunates. They must hurry with its building!

During the construction of the new hospital Dr. Schweitzer had a surprising and happy experience. He never lost an opportunity of telling people about his doctrine of Reverence for Life—the teaching that Life is sacred, even for harmless animals, and that we must never destroy it unless it is necessary. A poisonous snake which will kill human beings, or animals which must be killed for food are exceptions—but there was no reason for killing a harmless toad which had fallen into one of the holes made for the piles. So, when the natives saw the doctor lift out the toad before ramming down the stones or filling in the hole, they smiled at his weakness. But one day some of the Africans were clearing the bush and spotted a toad. Immediately one of them wanted to kill it but another—a real savage, according to Schweitzer—stopped him. Then he told the others what he had learned from the "old Doctor." It was that God made animals—even toads—just as He made men. Animals—even toads—had just as much right to life as men had. So, one day, God will hold a great palaver with men who kill or illtreat animals. The other Africans listened with respect, and the toad was left unharmed. None of them saw Dr. Schweitzer listening but he experienced a great happiness that even these primitive people could learn the great virtue of kindness to animals.

Throughout the whole of 1926 the work of building went on—but never for one moment did the medical and surgical work in the old buildings cease. Operations were performed, sleeping sickness patients treated and, when the disease had not gone too far, were cured. The scourge of dysentery slowly receded, babies were born (the white people living in that part of Africa would travel hundreds of miles so that their babies were born under Dr. Schweitzer's care), lepers were treated. Poor demented lunatics were calmed and even cured and the last hours of those who came to the hospital too late were passed in comfort and amidst kindness. Often, when evening came, Dr. Schweitzer was too tired even to hold a pen and concentrate on writing. His two white doctor colleagues worked just as hard as he did and so did the nurses. There was so much to be done—so many who needed help.

January 21st, 1927, was a red-letter day for everyone. It was the day on which the removal to the new hospital began. Canoes loaded with patients or hospital stores were towed upstream to the new buildings and then brought back for the next load. All day it went on and then, in the midst of it, a new patient—a white lady—arrived. But Dr. Schweitzer had foreseen this sort of emergency. There was a bed all ready for her. And so they progressed—more people, more stores, medicines and instruments. Last of all came the famous piano—a very difficult transportation for a dugout canoe. By evening the new hospital was filled, the old one deserted. Even the mental patients—who came quietly and gave no trouble—were safely installed in their new cells. These had wooden floors—dry and clean—a great improvement on the damp earth at the old hospital.

Just six months later Dr. Schweitzer decided that he could go home for a rest from all his arduous labors. He had been far from idle during those six months. The old hospital had been completely dismantled. Every piece of galvanized metal, every beam, every nail (even if they were bent they had to be hammered straight again) had to be salvaged. You can't afford to waste such things in the middle of the African forest. Then there was a dwelling house for the doctors to be built, together with the new hospital kitchen, a chicken house and a goat house—and a big shed for the canoes and boats. More helpers arrived from Europe during this time, including an English lady, Mrs. Russell, to take the place of others who had gone back home.

The group of new hospital buildings looked most impressive, all gleaming white in their new paint. Each one was constructed with an air space between the tops of the walls and the roof and they were thus much cooler than the old ones had been. The dysentery patients had a new isolation ward and the mental patients were well housed. One of them had arrived—in chains—at the hospital only a few months before. He was a fine-looking man named N'Tschambi who, in a sudden violent mad fit had attacked and killed a woman. In the hospital he had gradually become quieter and during his sane periods was even allowed to do some work. He would occasionally go with Mrs. Russell to help in clearing the bush or digging the gardens—a brave undertaking on her part. Whenever he felt a fit of madness about to possess him, he would go quietly, of his own accord, back to his cell.

It was N'Tschambi who was one of the last to see Dr. Schweitzer off on his journey back to Europe. He knew how much the doctor had done for him and so he asked, with anxiety in his heart, if the doctor had ordered that no one must send him away from the hospital in the doctor's absence? Schweitzer's answer brought tears of joy to N'Tschambi's eyes. "Certainly I have ordered it, N'Tschambi," he said.

"No one may send you away without first having a great palaver with me."

Another who was sad as he saw Schweitzer go was N'Tsama. He, too, had been insane, and he had also taken dysentery very badly. He was now cured of both, and in his thankfulness he remained to work at the hospital. "The doctor is my father and the hospital is my village," was N'Tsama's way of putting his feelings.

On July 29th, 1927, the ship which was taking Dr. Schweitzer and two of his nurses home for a rest left Cape Lopez and, for a while, Africa lost sight of him. It had been a sad parting. Although he looked forward so much to seeing his wife and daughter and friends again—and even though he was going to his beloved Gunsbach and Alsace—there was sorrow in leaving behind his hospital, his fellow workers and those people who, though at times they exasperated him, so fully trusted and depended upon their "old Doctor."

War Touches Lambaréné

A busy time awaited Schweitzer in Europe. His wife and his daughter Rhena had settled in Königsfeld, a little town in the Black Forest. He did not spend much time with them. He was off on his travels—lecturing and playing the organ— to raise money and to recruit help for his hospital. In the autumn and winter he went to Sweden, in the spring and summer he visited Holland and Britain, and then he went off to Czechoslovakia, Germany and Switzerland. There were hours of railway traveling (he always traveled third class—often in the reverse of comfort); practicing on strange organs before giving recitals, for he would never play on a strange organ to an audience without several previous hours of practice; interviews; lectures and, in what little time there was after all that, work on his new book, *The Mysticism of Paul the Apostle*. In fact, although the doctors had advised him to rest and take life easily, Schweitzer often resorted again to his old trick of sitting up all night, so that he might have absolute quiet for his writing. On those nights he would go to bed at six o'clock in the morning and get up again at ten.

At last the time for return to Lambaréné came. In December, 1929, he and his wife sailed from Bordeaux. He still had not finished his book on St. Paul so he made the final revisions and completed the last writing while aboard ship.

During the next ten years Dr. Schweitzer lived a busier life than most men half his age could have undertaken. On his third arrival at Lambaréné, in December, 1929, he was confronted by another severe epidemic of dysentery. Every available building had been pressed into service as an isolation ward and it was plain that yet more building was required. Once more the "old Doctor" turned his hand to constructing yet more extensions to the hospital. In due course they were erected. More patients could thus be treated. An English lady gave a very valuable necklace as her contribution to the hospital and the Necklace Building resulted.

A Swiss organist gave a series of concerts to raise money and another building, built with the proceeds, was named after her. So it went on and Dr. Schweitzer, now fifty-five years old, busied himself with the building work, took his share of medical duties, supervised the whole organization and wrote several more books!

In 1932 Dr. Schweitzer came back to Europe to deliver an address on Goethe as a part of the celebration of the 200th anniversary of the poet's birth. Once again, he could not escape a continual round of lectures and recitals. Everyone wanted to see and hear him. Everywhere he went he was honored and people flocked to hear him.

Then he went back to Lambaréné to his poor patients, to the little orphaned children who had been adopted and brought up by the hospital, and to his animal pets. On one occasion they took a census of the various animals which lived under the protection of Dr. Schweitzer, the lover of all animals. There were seven dogs, forty cats, six monkeys and numerous antelopes, goats, sheep, pelicans, chickens and ducks—and one porcupine! Two especial favorites of the doctor were Tchu-tchu, a dog which always sat behind his chair at mealtimes, although no other dog was allowed into the dining room, and Sisi, his cat. Sisi's mother had been stolen when she was but a tiny kitten, too young to be able to lap milk. Dr. Schweitzer, busy man as he was, took time to feed the kitten with a medicine dropper until she could lap for herself. When she grew up, Sisi, as cats will when there is some human who is particularly beloved by them, would sleep on the doctor's arm as he wrote in his study. She was never disturbed—even though her master had to manage his writing with one hand until she awoke.

In January, 1939, Dr. Schweitzer finished his sixth spell of work at Lambaréné and sailed for home. He was particularly looking forward to that visit because he was going to his old University city of Strassburg for a very special occasion. He had been made Honorary President of the Strassburg Festival for that year, and the entire program was to consist of the music of Bach. A great disappointment awaited him. With a very sorrowful heart he stayed for only a few days, did not wait for the Festival and did not even unpack his trunks. He saw what he had feared—that Europe was indeed on the verge of another outbreak of insanity—that war was inevitable. He took his wife and daughter to safety in Switzerland and exactly one month after leaving Africa he was in the same ship on her return voyage. If Europe was to be plunged into the war which the evil Hitler and his wicked associates were forcing upon it, then Schweitzer felt that his place was at Lambaréné.

As soon as he got back he commenced to work feverishly to build up his stocks of medicines, stores and supplies. He expended every cent the hospital possessed for he knew that when the war did come the flow of supplies would cease.

Once the news came that hostilities had indeed begun, Dr. Schweiter and his staff had to make a heart-rending decision. They did not know how long the war might last so they had to cut down on everything in order to conserve supplies.

Only the most serious cases could be kept at the hospital—the rest of the patients must be sent home. Because of the wickedness of the so-called civilized white men, the sick and suffering innocent people of Africa must go unrelieved. Poor sick Negroes must be deprived of the medicine and care which would make them better, because of what was happening in Europe. No wonder that Dr. Schweitzer considers that he and all who live in this world with him were born into an age of spiritual decadence!

And so, cut off from Europe as the German Nazis overran one country after another, the hospital at Lambaréné continued to function at less than one-quarter of its capacity. There were greater tribulations to come, however. The war actually reached Equatorial Africa and fighting took place in and around Lambaréné. When Germany defeated France and the puppet Government of Vichy was set up, certain Frenchmen refused to yield and established the Free French Government. It was the war between those two—Frenchman and Frenchman—which took place in Africa. Fortunately, although fighting took place in the village of Lambaréné itself, it did not reach the hospital. Both sides respected the work which Dr. Schweitzer was doing and he was left alone —although there was always the danger of stray shots, or even air raids. Finally, the Free French won and there was no more fighting.

The fighting around Lambaréné came to an end—but such was not the case with the hospital's difficulties. Nearly all of the European staff were called up for the armed forces and only four nurses and two doctors remained. Once more Schweitzer had to work as he had done right at the beginning—walking the wards, operating on the emergency cases which continued to come in, and controlling the entire establishment—hard work for a man of over sixty-five. Then, in August, 1941, what Dr. Schweitzer himself described as a near miracle occurred. A boat arrived from the coast and aboard was—Mrs. Schweitzer! Somehow she had managed to get to Africa—via Switzerland, France and Portugal—because she realized that her husband must be in need of all the help he could get. He was overjoyed to see her; while she, for her part, must have felt great anxieties for him. He was overworked and weary, but his tremendous spirit and great faith in God kept him going.

In December, 1940, Dr. Schweitzer had heard from friends in America that they were sending him a store of drugs and supplies for his hospital. This was indeed wonderful news but many, many times he must have wondered whether the news would ever be turned into reality. But patience was rewarded. In May, 1942—nineteen months later—the consignment arrived. What joy there was when it was unpacked! Not only had these warmhearted Americans provided a plentiful supply of drugs but there were various other supplies of all kinds. Some of the most welcome articles for Dr. Schweitzer himself were several pairs of rubber gloves. For a long time he had been using for operations gloves which were much too small for him—a very uncomfortable and difficult matter. Further consignments now began to reach the hospital from both America and England—the link with the outside world had not been altogether broken!

Two of those links were evident during 1945. On January 14th it was Dr. Schweitzer's seventieth birthday. Despite the fact that England was engaged in total war, the B.B.C. found time to broadcast a program in honor of that day. Far away in the African forest, with the noises of the jungle around them, Dr. Schweitzer and his wife heard a recording of some of Bach's organ music, played by the doctor himself on the organ of All Hallows, on Tower Hill, many years before. In 1945 All Hallows Church lay in ruins as a result of German bombs but the music of the recording lived and it brought joy to the heart of the man who made it.

On May 7th of that year one of the patients at the hospital heard, on his portable wireless set, that the war was over. He rushed to tell Dr. Schweitzer. That afternoon the hospital bell was rung and the glad news announced. It was a great relief to hear that the madness of war had, at last, ceased— but it was an utterly weary Dr. Schweitzer who heard the news and who dragged himself round his work that day. The one hope that kept him going, above all, was that some of the staff would now come back to Lambaréné and life would be easier. But he had long to wait. The first to arrive back at Lambaréné did not appear for over three months and it was not until 1948 that Dr. Schweitzer was able to leave the hospital and return home to Alsace. Except for those few days in 1939, he had been away for twelve years— living in a climate which is supposed to be impossible for

Europeans for more than two or three years! He was received with acclamation in Europe. Everyone had heard of the famous Dr. Schweitzer.

In 1949 Schweitzer went to America for the first time. He had promised to lecture over there and he felt a sense of gratitude to the American people who had so generously given to his hospital during the war. But there was something more than a lecture tour in this visit, something even more important than the large sums of money which the Americans subscribed for his hospital. He had heard that American scientists had discovered new drugs which would cure leprosy —and there were always lepers at the hospital at Lambaréné.

At the age of seventy-five Albert Schweitzer began to cure leprosy in Africa. In 1950 he had sixty patients with this disease and, by 1953, over 300. He made a separate lepers' village because there was no room at the hospital. He devoted his Nobel Peace Prize, as we mentioned at the beginning of this book, to proper buildings for these people—and word went round Equatorial Africa which kindled hope for people who before were condemned to slow death. "Leprosy can be cured. The old doctor can cure lepers!"

This, then, is the story of Albert Schweitzer, who so nobly practices as well as preaches the Christian life, and whose philosophy of "reverence for life" shines through his work, his writing and his music.

Author and Artist

John Merrett lives in London. He says his whole life has been a struggle between inherited characteristics. His father came from a long line of farmers; his mother's people have been seamen for centuries. He was born and educated in the English inland town of Reading and did not get to sea. But before he was twenty-one, he went to live on a small island in the Atlantic Ocean for ten years. From there he went to Belfast, Ireland, where he commenced his popular Children's Hour broadcasts. Since 1945 he has been a regular Children's Hour favorite. Young people, probably millions of them, have listened to his broadcasts and read his books. He has written many of them. He says his dual personality is reflected in his hobbies—gardening and fishing.

Parviz Sadighian was born in Tehran, Iran, in 1939. He was graduated from the Academy of Fine Arts in Tehran and received a partial scholarship for foreign study. In 1959 he enrolled at the Art Institute in Chicago and continued his studies in sculpture and in painting. Interest in painting led to courses in illustration and advertising art. Mr. Sadighian is now associated with the Bert Ray Studio in Chicago.

Index of Place Names

Africa, 14, 16, 17, 53, 54, 55, 57, 58, 61, 62, 65, 77, 82, 83, 88, 92, 95, 96, 97, 98, 110, 113, 123, 128, 131, 136, 137, 138, 140

Africa, Equatorial, 14, 16, 54, 61, 62, 83, 95, 123, 137, 140

Africa, French Equatorial, 14, 16, 54, 61, 62, 83, 95, 137, 140

Africa, West, 98

African forest, 86, 139

All Hallows Church, 139

Alsace, 19, 20, 27, 41, 58, 61, 65, 83, 89, 92, 94, 97, 119, 131, 139

Alsace, Lower, 41

America, 14, 125, 138, 139, 140

Atlantic Ocean, 62, 63

Balkan states, 30

Barcelona, 55, 94

Berlin, 30, 46, 54

Berne, 110

Birmingham, 97

Black Forest, the, 133

Bordeaux, 88, 93, 98, 134

Britain, 49, 133

Buckingham Palace, 13

Cambridge, 15, 97

Cameroon (Mt.), 99

Cape Lopez, 81, 131

Chicago, 15

Church of St. Nicholas, 47

Colmar, 17, 26, 54, 91, 92, 93

Colmar Museum, 26

Czechoslovakia, 96, 98, 134

Denmark, 96, 98

Douala, 99

Edinburgh, 15

England, 47, 96, 97, 98, 139

Equator, 58, 62

Equatorial Africa, 14, 16, 54, 61, 62, 83, 95, 123, 137, 140

Europe, 54, 70, 77, 82, 83, 84, 85, 87, 113, 125, 130, 133, 135, 136, 137, 140

Europe, Western, 15

France, 17, 20, 82, 89, 97, 98, 137, 138

French Equatorial Africa, 14, 16, 54, 61, 62, 83, 95, 137, 140

Garaison, 88, 89

Germany, 20, 27, 49, 82, 96, 134, 137

Gunsbach, 20, 21, 27, 33, 34, 40, 44, 59, 61, 89, 91, 92, 93, 97, 116, 131

Gunsbach Church, 33

Holland, 133

Ill, River, 39

Kayserberg, 19

Königsfeld, 133

Lambaréné, 58, 61, 62, 64, 65, 66, 69, 73, 81, 82, 83, 84, 88, 94, 96, 97, 98, 99, 100, 101, 103, 104, 108, 109, 113, 115, 118, 120, 134, 135, 136, 137, 139, 140

Le Havre, 58

London, 97

Mission (Roman Catholic), 70

Mission Station (Lambaréné), 64, 65, 69, 70, 74, 78, 99, 100, 101, 104, 106, 108, 120

Mulhausen, 27, 29, 31, 33, 34, 36

Mulhouse, 20, 27
Munich, 56
Norway, 15
Notre Dame Cathedral, 37
Ogowe, River, 58, 62, 64,
    67, 70, 74, 78, 97, 99,
    104, 107, 109
Oslo University, 15, 16
Oxford, 15, 97, 98
Paris, 37, 39, 45, 46, 54,
    55, 58, 84
Paris Conservatoire, 37
Portugal, 138
Prague, 15, 127
Pyrenees, 88
River Ill, 39
River Ogowe, 58, 62, 64,
    67, 70, 74, 78, 97, 99,
    104, 107, 109
Russia, 36
St. Andrews, 15
St. Nicholas, Church of,
    47, 57, 93, 96
St. Remy de Provence, 89
St. Stephen's Church, 33
St. Sulpice, 37
St. Thomas's College, 39,
    40, 41, 48, 55

St. William's Church, 45,
    56
Samkita, 74
Sorbonne, 45
Spain, 49, 96
Strassburg, 35, 39, 40, 41,
    45, 47, 58, 89, 93, 96,
    108, 136
Strassburg, University of,
    14, 36, 48, 50, 54, 55, 57,
    136
Sweden, 95, 96, 98, 112,
    133
Swedish Protestant
    Church, 94
Switzerland, 89, 96, 98,
    110, 127, 134, 136, 138
Tower Hill, 139
United States of America,
    14, 15
Uppsala, University of,
    94, 95
U.S.A., 14, 15
Washington, D.C., 14
West Africa, 98
Western Europe, 15
Zurich, 15, 97
Zurich University, 89

Credits

Designer/BERT RAY STUDIO

Illustrations by/PARVIZ SADIGHIAN

Cover Painting/MARY GEHR

Type/CALEDONIA

Paper/ 70# PUBLISHERS OFFSET

Printer/REGENSTEINER CORPORATION

DUE DATE

APR 0 8 1992			
			Printed in USA